FAUX SURFACES IN
POLYMER CLAY

FAUX SURFACES IN POLYMER CLAY

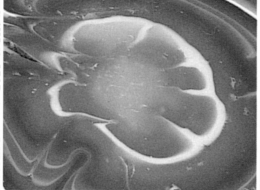

30 Techniques & Projects
That Imitate Precious Stones,
Metals, Wood & More

Irene Semanchuk Dean

LARK BOOKS
A Division of Sterling Publishing Co., Inc.
New York

EDITOR: Valerie Van Arsdale Shrader
ART DIRECTOR: Kathleen Holmes
PHOTOGRAPHER: Evan Bracken
ADDITIONAL COVER PHOTOGRAPHY: keithwright.com
COVER DESIGNER: Barbara Zaretsky
ILLUSTRATIONS: Lorelei Buckley
ASSISTANT EDITOR: Heather Smith
PRODUCTION ASSISTANCE: Lorelei Buckley
EDITORIAL ASSISTANCE: Delores Gosnell
Rosemary Kast

DEDICATION
For Scott, always.

Library of Congress Cataloging in Publication Data
Dean, Irene Semanchuk.
    Faux surfaces in polymer clay : 30 techniques & projects that imitate precious stones,
metals, wood & more / Irene Semanchuk Dean.
        p.   cm.
    Includes index.
    ISBN 1-57990-408-4
    1. Polymer clay craft.   I. Title.
TT297.D375 2003
731.4'2—dc21

                                    2003000519

10 9 8 7 6 5 4 3 2 1

Published by Lark Books, a division of Sterling Publishing Co., Inc.
387 Park Avenue South, New York, N.Y. 10016

© 2003, Irene Semanchuk Dean

Distributed in Canada by Sterling Publishing,
c/o Canadian Manda Group, 165 Dufferin Street
Toronto, Ontario, Canada M6K 3H6

Distributed in the U.K. by Guild of Master Craftsman Publications Ltd., Castle Place, 166 High Street, Lewes,
East Sussex, England BN7 1XU Tel: (+ 44) 1273 477374, Fax: (+ 44) 1273 478606, Email:
pubs@thegmcgroup.com, Web: www.gmcpublications.com

Distributed in Australia by Capricorn Link (Australia) Pty Ltd., P.O. Box 704, Windsor, NSW 2756 Australia

If you have questions or comments about this book, please contact:
Lark Books
67 Broadway
Asheville, NC 28801
(828) 253-0467

Manufactured in China

ISBN 1-57990-408-4

Contents

INTRODUCTION

IF YOU HAVE SOME experience working with polymer clay, you've probably experimented with imitative techniques a bit; perhaps you'd like to perfect the ones you're already using, or maybe you'd like to learn to create some new faux surfaces. I've been working with polymer clay for over 10 years, and I still get excited about learning new techniques and developing new ways to use them to express myself in this fabulous medium. So I've gathered recipes from a dozen talented polymer clay artists, added a few of my own, and I present 30 of them now to you. These remarkable techniques imitate gemstones, metals, and other natural materials, and rival the originals in luster, brilliance, and beauty.

Polymer clay can simulate a multitude of surfaces, from the sleek sparkle of tiger-eye to the industrial grittiness of rusted steel. The colors, texture, and versatility of this material make it perfect for creating faux surfaces. Blend the colors to produce the perfect deep blue for lapis lazuli or the rich red of cinnabar. Polish the clay smooth to re-create mother-of-pearl, or texture it roughly to mimic bone or ivory. It's pliable enough to become anything from a simple spacer bead to a pair of exotic candlesticks. Fold it, texture it, stamp it, sand it, drill it, glue it, bake it, and bake it again—there are an infinite number of ways that polymer clay can be manipulated to achieve the imitative effect you desire.

I'll also explore the results achieved through the use of specific types of polymer clay. For instance, certain recipes utilize the effects of the

mica powders inherent in some of the metallic polymer clays, while others exploit the properties of the
translucent clays. Paints, inks, mica powders, wax
compounds, and confetti can enhance the surface of the
clay to add the sparkle of an opal or the sheen of silver.
Proper sanding and buffing can help create the brilliant shine that
defines many of these natural substances.

The book features a diverse selection of techniques, with five
categories of faux surfaces. In addition to metals, precious gems,
and stones, there's also a section on natural materials, such as
amber and wood. You'll see a number of recipes that simulate
specific surface decoration techniques, such as dichroic glass, cloisonné, and basse-taille enamel. Not only will you find step-by-step,
illustrated instructions for creating each faux surface, but you'll also
be treated to beautiful projects designed by the recipe contributors,
each and every one of them a gifted polymer clay artist. The
book has been arranged so you can use the recipes to follow your muse and create the projects with any kind of imitative surface you choose. It's technique-driven, so you can
apply the process in any number of ways.

Although I've included many recipes here, please
consider these to be just the start of your adventure with imitative techniques. Use this book to
inspire your own explorations and experiments with polymer clay.
Enjoy the journey.

Beads and artifacts by
Irene Semanchuk Dean

MATERIALS, TOOLS & TECHNIQUES

You'll need a variety of materials to create imitative surfaces. In addition to clay, you may use inks, paints, leafing pens, colored pencils, foils, glitters, and liquid clay.

Although you're familiar with the fundamental properties of polymer clay, I'm including some basic information as a reference. Some of the following is rather general, but much of it can be applied specifically to the creation of imitative surfaces. Each recipe will include detailed information for its particular surface.

Materials

Since the creation of a successful faux requires the proper combination of a number of elements—the right color or brand of clay, the correct inclusions or surface decoration—the following section offers some advice about using these materials.

Polymer clay. There are several different brands of polymer clay available on the market, and each has its own unique properties that can be important when you're creating a faux technique. Each handles slightly differently prior to baking, and each has its own post-baking strength and flexibility. A few examples: Sculpey III is easy to work with but sometimes fragile after baking, while Cernit is great for sculpting because it blends well at seams. Premo! Sculpey and Kato Polyclay use mica powders for their metallic clays; these ingredients enable surface techniques that just aren't possible in clays that don't have them. I'll discuss these properties in more depth on page 13.

Experiment with several brands to decide which is right for your work style and your aesthetic. Each manufacturer offers a variety of colors, and you can custom blend them to create your own shades, which you'll often need to do to create an accurate imitative surface. Some of the recipes in this book call for a specific brand; in some cases, this is because a certain color or property is required for the accurate simulation of a surface. If no brand name is mentioned, feel free to use your favorite brand of clay. See page 142 for information about suppliers if you can't find a specific product in your area.

Liquid polymer clay. By now you've probably experimented a bit with liquid polymer clay. It's a terrific medium for making nearly transparent transfers, as in the faux basse-taille enamel project on page 125. It can be tinted with oil paints or mica powders and used to fill cells for faux cloisonné (see page 114), or used as a glaze (see the celadon project page 103). Some people find that liquid polymer clay bakes clearer when the temperature is bumped to 300°F (150°C) for a few minutes. Use reasonable caution when baking, because it creates fumes and the fumes increase as the temperature does.

Liquid polymer clay can also be used like glue: since it's made of the same substance as polymer clay, it creates a superior bond between two pieces. Your pieces must, of course, be baked after you've applied the liquid clay.

Mica powders. These are extremely fine flakes of colored mica, and they add a metallic shine to the surface of polymer clay. While they can be physically mixed into the clay (usually into translucent clay to achieve the greatest effect), they're generally used on the surface. When spread with a finger or a dry paintbrush, these powders will stick to the surface of the clay. I always wear a dust mask when working with mica powders to avoid breathing the fine particles, which easily become airborne. Normally, mica powder must be sealed with a varnish after baking to prevent it from rubbing off.

Inks and paints. Permanent transparent alcohol-based inks can be used to tint polymer clay, and other inks are used to stamp the clay's surface to embellish faux surfaces such as jade. Paints are often added to layers of clay to create effects such as the bands in agate.

Several recipes, like the bone directions on page 59, use acrylic paint as a stain. Although the surface instructions provide

Making transfers with liquid polymer clay

Tinting clay with inks

more specific details, essentially you apply acrylic paint to baked polymer clay (using your fingers to press the paint into every nook and cranny), and then wipe off the excess paint. Once the paint is dry, you can sand the polymer clay to remove the paint on the higher surfaces. Thinning paint with water will create a wash, which is an appropriate method to achieve a specific simulation; read the copper verdigris recipe on page 53 for more information.

Occasionally, you'll see a specific brand or color of paint, ink, or other material listed in the recipe. As with the clays, some artists have indicated that the properties of a particular product—its translucency, heat resistance, etc.—are required to create the desired effects in the faux surface.

Inclusions. Glitter, confetti, and metal leaf are used in several recipes that require decorative elements. Look at the dichroic glass recipe on page 106 to see how beautifully glitter and leaf are used, and a little bit of confetti goes a long way in simulating the iridescence of opal on page 32.

Wax paper or deli paper. Many polymer clay artists like to create a moveable work surface

with these materials. You can remove the clay from the paper with little or no distortion by carefully peeling the paper from the back of the clay.

Wax paper and deli paper also help prevent a brayer or acrylic rod from sticking to the clay; just place the paper on top of the clay surface first. Crumpled wax paper can also be used to impart texture, as you'll see in the slate recipe on page 87.

Mold releases. If you're using a mold, you need something to prevent the clay from sticking to the mold. Water is a suitable mold release, as is the non-aerosol spray-on vinyl protectant available at automotive parts stores. Cornstarch is also an excellent mold release, but it can leave residue that's difficult to remove after baking. Look to each recipe for more specific information on using these products.

Glues. When you want to cover an object that polymer clay doesn't want to stick to, such as wood or metal, first coat the object with heat-resistant polyvinyl acetate (PVA) white glue. Allow the glue to dry before covering the object, and polymer clay will adhere to it nicely.

Iridescent glitter and confetti give the faux opal its glimmer.

Though cyanoacrylate glue will not hold its bond through the baking process, it's perfect for gluing polymer clay projects after they have been baked. Swipe the areas to be glued with an alcohol-soaked cotton ball to remove any oils. Follow the glue manufacturer's guidelines, and be sure to ventilate well when you're using this product.

Varnishes. These finishes are necessary to protect a surface element that may otherwise rub off, such as mica powders or metal leaf. Although varnishes are manufactured by the same companies that produce polymer clay, some suitable alternatives include certain floor polishes and water-based acrylic finishes; see the supplier's note on page 142 for details on how to obtain these products. Some varnishes, including most clear nail polishes, will react with the clay and cause it to become sticky over time, so be sure to use only a polymer-friendly varnishing product. You can also use varnishes to give a high gloss to a surface if you don't have a buffing wheel.

Here's a tip: Apply two or more thin coats of varnish, instead of one heavy coat, to obtain smoother results.

The tools you'll use include rollers, brayers, wet/dry sandpaper or sponges, sculpting tools, cutting blades, shape cutters, texturing tools, and of course, a pasta machine.

Tools

You've probably amassed a collection of polymer clay tools, and there are no doubt some you use all the time. Here's a quick rundown of the essentials, plus a few extras that will be helpful in making faux surfaces.

Pasta machine. This isn't exactly a must, but it's pretty close. Not only does it assist in conditioning clay, it rolls uniformly thin sheets of clay that can't be achieved as quickly or perfectly with a brayer or roller. At its thinnest settings, a pasta machine can also roll paper-thin clay sheets, which is a necessary step for some of the recipes in

Molds and stamps are handy in creating a variety of the projects included here.

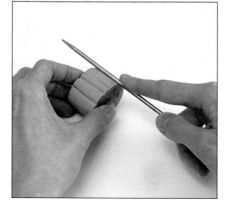

Knitting needles can be useful tools for creating faux surfaces.

this book. Learn to roll ultra-thin sheets of clay on page 14.

Some polymer clay artists like to use a "stripped-down" pasta machine; that is, one that has had its housing removed—this allows access to the back side of the rollers for quick cleaning. The housing is not structurally important, and can be removed without compromising the performance or safety of the machine. It'll take just a quick search on the internet to find instructions for disassembling, cleaning, and reassembling your pasta machine.

Brayer or acrylic rod. In addition to a pasta machine, you'll need these tools for flattening the clay. Some artists use rolling pins, too.

Food processor. This machine is used in several recipes to chop the clay into small pieces; it helps create the proper texture for the faux cork on page 65, for example. Be sure to run it in short bursts while you work.

Cutting tools. There are blades sold specifically for polymer clay, but surgical tissue blades or paint scraper blades also work very well. A craft knife will be best for some types of cutting. The

surface directions will specify a particular cutting utensil if it's really necessary; otherwise, you should use the tool with which you feel most comfortable. After every few cuts, wipe your blade on a paper towel with a bit of rubbing alcohol to clean it.

Miscellaneous tools. Needle tools, steel weaving needles, and knitting needles are all good tools, and a necessity if you plan to make beads. Bamboo skewers work well, too, but it can be difficult to remove clay that has been baked on the skewer. Sculpting tools will be invaluable for a variety of things, especially for some of the faux techniques that require random indentations or markings; look for these in the ceramics section of a well-stocked craft supply store. You can also use found objects, such as credit cards, golf tees, crochet hooks, or cuticle shapers, and you can make your own custom shaping-coaxing-nudging tools from—you guessed it—polymer clay.

You can carve baked polymer clay with a gouge, sold in craft stores as a linoleum block cutter. (See page 16 for more details about carving.) This is a good alternative or addition to using molds in various faux techniques.

You'll notice that molded polymer clay has gentler edges than carved polymer; keep this difference in mind while you're working on a faux surface.

Molds and texture sheets.
Molds and texture sheets are used in several of the projects that follow. Commercial molds are available at craft stores, but I find it much more satisfying to use ones that I've made. (See page 14 for more details about making your own molds.) Texture sheets are also commercially available, but consider found objects such as window screen or textured wallpaper, or even make your own.

Clay gun. In the Balinese silver recipe included here, decorative coils and spirals are created from lengths of clay that are extruded from the gun.

Buffing wheel. You may need this tool to create shine, depending upon the surface you create. Read more about buffing on page 16, and don't skip the information on safety found on page 17.

Techniques

There are a few processes you should be familiar with before you begin to practice imitative techniques. As you examine the recipes, you'll see that some fauxs are achieved before the clay is baked, some after, and some, well, in between.

Before Baking
Besides proper conditioning, you may also need to utilize some specific rolling techniques, leach the clay, or make a mold before you bake.

Conditioning
Since you're an experienced polymer clay user, you already know that you need to condition your clay, and you know how to do it and why—conditioning thoroughly mixes the components of the clay. It's also the perfect time to create the custom color blends that you'll need in many of the following recipes.

Aligning the Mica Particles
You'll find a couple of references to aligning mica particles in the recipes ahead. The metallic clays mentioned on page 8 contain mica powders, and you'll notice the changeable luster when you alter the angle at which you view the clay. This property has been

The luster of this tiger-eye imitation results from the mica luster in the gold metallic clay.

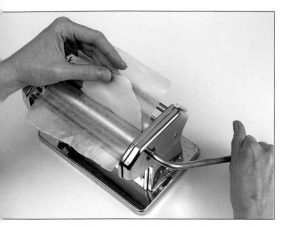

Rolling an extra-thin sheet of polymer clay

Note the excess plasticizers that have been leached into the paper.

well utilized in the execution of some of the faux techniques in this book, like tiger-eye and mother-of-pearl.

The mica particles are aligned when the surface of a sheet of metallic clay appears to be a uniform color. To achieve this, feed the clay through the pasta machine repeatedly, always folding it and feeding it back through in the same direction. After 10 to 12 passes, the surface should appear to be one smooth color.

Rolling Paper-Thin Sheets of Clay

Create these by placing a thin sheet of clay between two pieces of wax paper and rolling it through a pasta machine. There are a few tricks to this process: first, roll the clay as thin as possible without using wax paper. Next, place it between two pieces of wax paper, but press only on the leading edge that you'll feed into the pasta machine first. As you start to feed in that edge, allow the clay to separate from the paper above the rollers, as shown at top left. Since the clay isn't constrained by the paper, the rolling action is smooth and the clay has room to expand into a very thin sheet. Carefully peel the wax paper away from the clay to use these paper-thin sheets.

Leaching

Some recipes, like the cork directions on page 65, call for leaching the clay to remove the excess plasticizer. Roll the unconditioned clay into a sheet and place it between two pieces of paper. Weight it with a tile (not a book, because the plasticizer may damage the cover) until the paper has absorbed some of the plasticizer, at which time you'll see an oily residue on the paper. This can take just a few hours, or it may need to leach overnight. In most cases, you'll need to condition the clay afterward to thoroughly mix the remaining plasticizer into the clay body. Some of the soft clays tend to get mushy when they're handled, so they benefit from leaching, too.

Making a Mold or Texture Sheet

To make your own molds or texture sheets, blend scrap polymer clay until it's a uniform color. For a mold, shape the clay into a slightly flattened circle a bit thicker than the item you're molding; for a texture sheet, roll the polymer clay into a sheet at a medium setting on your pasta machine. Apply a generous amount of release directly to the object you're using as the basis for the mold or sheet, and press it slowly, firmly, and straight down into the polymer clay. Pull gently to release it, and bake the clay mold or texture sheet for an hour at the manufacturer's recommended temperature. (A longer baking time will result in a stronger mold.)

During Baking

Of course you know that most brands of polymer clay bake at 275°F (136°C), but be sure to check the package of the brand you buy. Polymer clay must have the proper baking temperature—too low and the piece won't cure properly, too high and it will burn. Buy an inexpensive oven thermometer and use it.

Although package directions usually indicate an amount of time per ¼ inch (6 mm) of thickness, I bake for a minimum of 30 minutes no matter how small or thin the piece, and up to an hour for thicker, larger pieces. If a piece isn't baked long enough, the polymer may not have a chance to fuse completely, resulting in a weak finished piece. Baking for a longer time does no harm, as long as the temperature remains where it should.

Tenting

If you're concerned about fumes, bake in a covered baking dish, or *tent* your polymer clay with aluminum foil. (The latter is also recommended when baking in a toaster oven, because it protects the clay from the close heating elements.) The ideal baking situation would be a dedicated convection oven, at a window, with an exhaust fan.

Tenting with aluminum foil can also minimize darkening, which can be a concern with some of the reds and the translucents used to create faux surfaces.

Plaquing

All of the translucent clays and some of the lighter colors in a few brands are susceptible to something called *plaquing*. Plaquing appears after the clay is baked, when small, white, crescent-shaped marks appear just under the surface of the clay. For some imitative techniques, such as jade or quartz, plaquing is not necessarily a bad thing and can enhance the realism of a surface. However, it's very disappointing to make the perfect faux opals only to have them plaque in the oven.

The creation of plaquing is not a precise science! Some people swear that the moisture on their hands imparted to the clay increases its likelihood. For that reason, you may want to handle your translucents as little as

This piece of faux amber exhibits plaquing.

Carving is an effective technique to use in creating imitative surfaces, especially stones.

Some fauxs require just a gentle buffing as a finishing touch.

possible if you don't want them to plaque. Temperature shocks also seem to cause plaquing; to prevent them, put the clay in a cold oven and bring it up to the correct temperature. When the baking time has elapsed, turn off the oven and crack the door slightly to allow the clay to cool slowly. Of course, if you want to increase the plaquing in your faux jade pendant, preheat the oven and remove the piece immediately after baking.

After Baking

There are a few ways you can embellish your imitative surfaces after baking.

Carving

Carving baked polymer clay results in a look that can't be achieved any other way. Carved lines have more abrupt edges than stamped lines, and thus more realistically imitate some carved gemstones. A linoleum gouge can easily carve through baked polymer clay; draw an image or design directly onto the polymer surface to guide your carving. To make smooth curved lines, move the clay in the direction of the curve while holding the gouge steady.

Sanding and Buffing

Some imitative techniques require sanding and even buffing

to attain the most realism. Always sand polymer clay with wet/dry sandpaper (available at auto parts stores) to both prevent polymer dust from becoming airborne and to keep the sandpaper from scratching the clay. It's not necessary to sand under water, but you should keep the clay and the sandpaper wet at all times. If you work in a bowl of water, as opposed to under water, you'll conserve natural resources. Never skip successive grits of paper. Depending on how smooth your piece is after baking, you can start as low as 320 or 400 grit, and work your way up to 800 or even 1,500 grit.

Sanding without subsequent buffing will create a smooth surface with a dull shine. Buffing a sanded piece with a rag (a piece of worn denim is perfect) will bring up a subtle sheen or luster, which is appropriate for the gleam of textured leather or carved cinnabar. A high shine, necessary for gemstones like malachite or tiger-eye, can be achieved by buffing on a cotton wheel attached to a bench grinder or jeweler's buffer. A hand-held rotary tool can sometimes be an adequate substitute for a buffing wheel, but be aware that a little pressure goes a long way. It's easy to gouge the clay with the tiny, high-speed wheel, so proceed with caution.

Imitative techniques are more effective when the degree of shine is accurate, so choose your finishing method accordingly. See the buffing sidebar at right for instructions and important safety tips.

Safety

Polymer clay artists know that the material is certified non-toxic, but there are still some common sense precautions you should take, and it's not a bad idea to be reminded of these important safeguards. If you use kitchen tools for polymer clay they shouldn't be used for food again, and don't allow any objects made from polymer clay to come into contact with food.

Polymer clay leaves a residue on your hands while you work with it. Many people clean up with pre-moistened, alcohol-based hand wipes, but my preference is hand lotion. The lotion seems to break down the polymer clay and I rub it off with a rough terrycloth rag. After that, I scrub with soap and a nailbrush to remove all traces from my knuckles and fingernails.

Don't breathe polymer fumes while baking—use an exhaust fan. Continued use of an oven for polymer clay will result in a coating of oily film on the oven walls. (Although a dedicated oven is ideal, it's not always practical.) Either wipe down the oven after baking polymer clay (I prefer to use water and baking soda for a mild abrasive), or bake in a dedicated covered roasting pan. A suitable alternative would be to cover your baking tray with aluminum foil.

BUFFING SAFETY

Practice caution when buffing! The wheel moves at an extremely high speed. Before you even turn on the motor, tie back any long hair, and remove necklaces or dangling bracelets. It's also advisable to wear eye protection and a dust mask, since tiny bits of cotton fiber from the wheel become airborne while buffing. Always hold your polymer clay piece next to the underside of the wheel when buffing—if it gets snatched from your fingertips (and this happens more often than you might think), it will shoot away from

you instead of toward you. Make certain that there are no children, pets, windows, or fragile things in the line of fire. Constantly move your piece—holding it in one place against the wheel will result in friction that can begin to melt the clay.

Learn a new skill, like simple bookmaking, while you employ a faux technique.

Using This Book

In addition to my own work, I've also included the work of 12 polymer clay artists whom I admire. We're calling our surface instructions "recipes," because we intend that you interpret them as you would directions in a cookbook—you can follow the recipes precisely if you wish, or improvise a little if you're feeling adventurous. In fact, a few of the artists who contributed recipes had a difficult time writing them, because they tinker with their recipes every time they use them! We hope you'll apply your own creativity to the ideas we've suggested here—make your faux turquoise a little more green, or turn our faux bronze into your faux gold.

Along the same lines, bear in mind that the artists who contributed these recipes have a favorite brand of clay, ink, paint, or what have you. Though they have found that these recipes work as written, feel free to experiment with your preferred materials. Doubtless, you know that not all products are compatible with polymer clay, so bear that in mind if you make any substitutions.

When you examine the recipes, you'll find that each one is a complete guide to the creation of the surface. Although basic baking times are included in the recipes, you may need to alter these depending upon the kind of project that you create with the surface; beads may need to bake longer than a thin sheet, for example. Following each recipe is a project featuring that surface. I separated the recipe from the project deliberately, so you can feel free to adapt the surface to any project you like. For instance, maybe you'd prefer to have jade bookends, rather than cinnabar ones? Adapt the jade surface recipe to the bookend project, and *voilà*. The book is organized to allow you the freedom to explore these imitative techniques to your heart's content.

And, when you study the projects, you'll see that many require skills that are in your repertoire already, such as covering an object, making a lid, or creating an inlay. But the projects may present you with the opportunity to learn a new technique, like fashioning a simple book, making a clock, or even sculpting. Finally, look to the gallery for inspiration: it features the work of some of the most highly regarded polymer clay artists working in the medium today.

I

Gemstones

MALACHITE

Create the distinctive concentric rings of rich green found in malachite with three different color mixtures and a little manipulation.

RECIPE CONTRIBUTED BY **Pat Laukkonen**

Materials

Premo!—Black, Sea Green, and White

Wet/dry sandpaper—400 through 800 or 1,000 grit

Tools

Pasta machine

Cutting blade

Smooth round tool, like a knitting needle

Brayer

Buffing wheel

Instructions

1 Use three different shades of green. To make the darkest color, use 2 parts sea green + 1 part black. For the medium color, use sea green only. For the lightest shade, add equal parts sea green and white.

2 Make two bull's-eye canes with the darkest color in the center; vary the thickness of the sheets and the arrangement of the shades of green. Use many layers, from thin to medium thickness. Make both of these bull's-eye canes approximately the same size.

3 Put the two canes together side by side. Make some very thin bull's-eye canes that are different from one another and place them in the spaces between the larger canes, as shown.

4 Stack several thin layers of different shades of green into a sheet, large enough to wrap the bull's-eye cane assembly you created in the previous step. Wrap the assembly with the layered sheet and butt the edges.

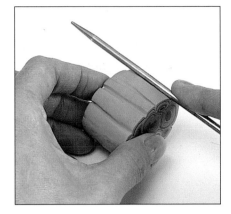

5 Use a smooth, round tool (like a knitting needle) to press the outer wrapped layer into the dents between the logs; it should mold to the canes. Don't leave gaps or air spaces between the inner logs and this layer. Add another slightly different layer, if you like.

6 Cut slices from the faux malachite cane and cover your project. Arrange them randomly on the surface, roll with a brayer to smooth, and bake according to manufacturer's instructions.

7 When cool, wet-sand with 400- through 800- or 1,000-grit sandpaper. Buff for shine.

makeup set

Now your cosmetic brushes can be a handsome reflection on you. Faux malachite handles transform your beauty tools into things of beauty themselves.

Materials

Premo!—Sea Green

Cosmetic brushes of various sizes

Translucent liquid polymer clay or heat-resistant PVA white glue

Polymer clay—black (optional)

Tools

Pasta machine

Cutting blade

Needle tool or similar thin object

MALACHITE RECIPE ON PAGE 20

Instructions

1. Roll a sheet of sea green polymer clay to a medium thickness on your pasta machine.

2. Take thin slices of the faux malachite log you made from the recipe and place them on the sheet of green clay. When you are happy with the arrangement, run it through the pasta machine on the thickest setting.

3. Roll the sheet of clay through two or three incrementally thinner settings on the pasta machine, rotating the sheet 90° between passes through the machine to prevent distortion.

4. Place the clay on your work surface with the malachite pattern facing down. Slice one side to make a straight edge. Place the handle of the makeup brush on the clay so the straight edge is touching the end of the handle nearest the bristles. Slice the clay just above the other end of the handle, leaving barely enough to fold over the end.

5. Roll the clay around the handle until it meets and mark the spot, cutting just inside your mark. Cover the handle with a thin layer of liquid clay or glue, and roll the clay onto the handle so the seams butt and don't overlap.

6. Smooth the seam delicately until it is nearly invisible. Roll gently on your work surface to make firm contact with the brush handle. Score the clay with a needle tool or similar straight object, as shown on the thinner brush.

7. Bake following the manufacturer's instructions. (To create the band on the thicker brush, fill the scored area with a strip of black clay after the first baking, and bake again.) Sand and buff to a high shine as indicated in the recipe.

LAPIS LAZULI

The regal look of lapis lazuli—
with its flecks of gold—is easily
imitated with blue clays, bronze
mica powder, and gold leaf.

RECIPE CONTRIBUTED BY **Dawn Schiller**

Materials

**Premo!—Cobalt Blue and
    Ultramarine Blue**

Metal leaf—gold

Mica powder—bronze

**Wet/dry sandpaper—400 and
    600 grit (optional)**

**Polymer-friendly varnish—
    glossy (optional)**

Tools

Pasta machine

**Buffing wheel or soft cloth
    (optional)**

Instructions

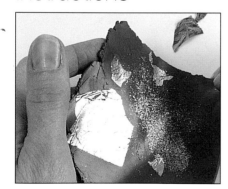

1 Mix 1 part cobalt blue clay
    + 2 parts ultramarine clay

in the pasta machine. Put random bits of bronze mica powder and gold leaf on the sheet of clay, and keep folding and rolling through the pasta machine.

2 Continue to add more leaf to the blend, until the flecks of metallic color are distributed in a pleasing manner. Buff the surface smooth with your finger and just a tiny bit of water.

3 Bake according to the manufacturer's directions. If your finished surface is simple, wet-sand with 400-, then 600-grit sandpaper as shown; buff with a soft cloth or buffing wheel. However, if your completed project is sculpted, smooth with your finger as in step 2 and skip the sanding and buffing. After baking a sculpted project, finish with varnish for a high gloss, if appropriate.

drawer pulls

Use these special accessories to create a luxurious ambiance in your home. These drawer pulls exude the unmistakable allure of lapis lazuli.

Materials

**Round drawer pulls
  (porcelain is ideal)**

Tools

Pasta machine

Ruler

Cutting blade

Circle cutter

LAPIS LAZULI RECIPE ON PAGE 24

Instructions

1. Roll the lapis lazuli blend through the second thickest setting of the pasta machine. The sheet needs to be long enough to wrap around the "neck" portion of the drawer pull.

2. Measure the drawer pull against the clay sheet and cut a strip wide enough to cover the neck from the base to top of the pull, and long enough to wrap around it once. Wrap the strip of clay around the neck of the drawer pull, stretching gently. Cut darts, if necessary, to work the clay upward onto the curve of the handle. Form butt edges and smooth the seams together with a finger or clay tool.

3. Use a circle cutter to cut a piece of clay that is slightly larger than the face of the drawer pull and lay it on the face, being careful to work out all the air bubbles. Smooth the seams where the clay on the face joins the clay you wrapped around the drawer pull in step 2.

4. Smooth out any fingerprints on the clay. Add more bits of gold leaf and bronze mica powder, if desired, and smooth into the clay.

5. Bake according to the manufacturer's directions.

6. When the pulls are cool, sand and buff as directed in the surface instructions.

PROJECT BY **Dawn Schiller**

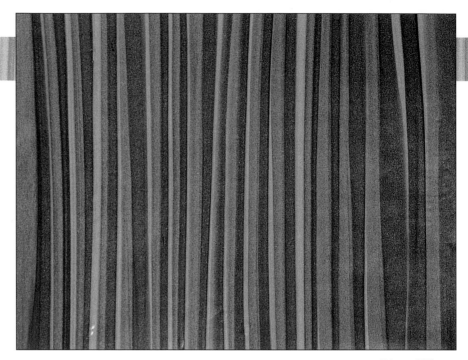

TIGER-EYE

This lustrous simulation of tiger-eye results from the mica effect in the gold polymer clay.

RECIPE CONTRIBUTED BY **Diane Villano**

Materials

Premo!—Gold, Black, Pearl, Green, and Translucent

Wet/dry sandpaper—400 through 1,000 grit

Polymer-friendly varnish— glossy

Tools

Craft knife or cutting blade

Pasta machine

Paintbrush

Instructions

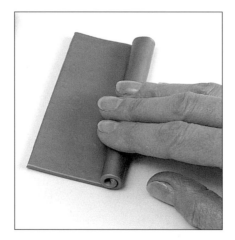

1 Start with the gold clay and add a tiny bit of black, pearl, and green. Make two more gold mixtures, adding a bit more black each time. Separately roll each mix through the pasta machine on the thickest setting, folding and re-rolling until the mica particles are aligned and the clay sheet is shiny. Roll each sheet into a cylinder, as shown, being careful to avoid air pockets.

2 Condition the translucent clay and roll into three very thin cylinders, roughly one third to one quarter the diameter of the gold mixtures, but with the same length.

3 Place the three gold cylinders together lengthwise. Add the translucent cylinders between the gold as shown.

4 Twist the gold/translucent bundle from each end, as shown. Continue to twist until the strips of color are very fine. Roll the bundle on your work surface until it's fairly smooth.

5 Pinch one edge of the bundle along the length, so in cross section, it resembles a teardrop, as the photo shows. Place the pinched edge in the pasta machine and roll through at the thickest setting. Roll through thinner settings until the sheet is thin and flexible.

6 Bake according to the manufacturer's instructions and let cool.

7 Sand with wet/dry sandpaper. Be sure to change the water frequently, after each or every second grit change.

8 Brush on a light coat of a glossy polymer-friendly varnish and let dry. Repeat with another coat, if desired.

Alternative: Instead of using varnish, buff to a deep shine.

pair of candlesticks

A memorable table setting wouldn't be complete without flickering candlelight. It's particularly bewitching when reflected from faux tiger-eye, with its shining metallic bands.

Materials

Wooden or metal candlestick forms

Heat-resistant PVA white glue

Acrylic paint—black

Tools

Paintbrushes

Craft knife or cutting blade

TIGER-EYE RECIPE ON PAGE 26

Instructions

1. Brush a thin coat of glue on the part of the candlesticks you'll cover with clay. Let them dry to a light tackiness.

2. Cut a strip from the sheet of faux tiger-eye that's the same width as the length of the area to be covered, and long enough to go completely around it. Roll the clay strip around the candlestick forms, being very careful not to trap air pockets between the form and the clay. Working from the widest part of the form, gradually press the clay to the form and work your way out to the ends. Trim the excess clay with your craft knife or cutting blade. Butt the edges and smooth the seam by pressing gently with your finger.

3. Bake the candlesticks according to the manufacturer's instructions and let them cool.

4. Sand and finish the surface according to the recipe. If you wish, paint the exposed sections of the candlesticks, as shown here.

PROJECT BY **Diane Villano**

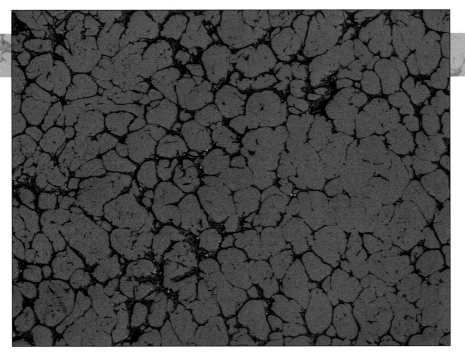

TURQUOISE

Use a common ingredient from your garden—dirt!—to help create the realistic-looking veins and fissures found in true turquoise.

RECIPE CONTRIBUTED BY **Irene Semanchuk Dean**

Materials

Polymer clay—turquoise blue, orange, and ecru or light beige

Small amount of dirt

Sculpey Diluent

Paper towels

Acrylic paint—burnt umber

Wet/dry sandpaper—400 through 1,000 grit

Bowl of water

Tools

Food processor

Buffing wheel

Instructions

1 Since most turquoise blue polymer clays are too bright to simulate real turquoise, add a pinch of orange to the turquoise to decrease the brightness, and a pinch of ecru or light beige to mute the color slightly. Mix thoroughly.

2 Tear the polymer clay into ½-inch (1.3 cm) pieces and toss them into the food processor. Chop in short bursts until the clay has formed irregularly shaped balls. Empty them onto your work surface.

3 Shape as desired, depending upon your final project. As you shape, leave fissures and small gaps visible. If you're rolling the clay into a bead shape or pressing it into a mold, apply enough pressure so the clay sticks to itself, but not so much that all of the fissures disappear.

4 Bake at 275°F (136°C) for 30 to 40 minutes.

5 When completely cool, mix a small amount of dirt with a few drops of diluent to create a muddy substance. Apply this to the surface of the clay with your fingers, as shown, forcing it into the fissures and gaps, and completely filling the larger gaps. The dirt contains particles of mica flakes that will impart realistic veining. Wipe away any excess from the surface with a paper towel; wipe gently to avoid scratching the surface of the clay with the particles in the muddy mixture.

6 Apply burnt umber paint to the surface of the clay, rubbing it into the muddy mixture in the fissure lines. Wipe off the excess paint with a paper towel. Allow to dry completely, then bake again for 10 minutes at 275°F (136°C).

7 When cool, wet-sand the polymer clay with 400- through 800- or 1,000-grit sandpaper. Dunk the paper in water instead of immersing the clay, to prevent the dirt from getting too wet. Buff gently to finish.

mayan face wall hanging

Create your own artifact to honor the achievements of the Mayans, who treasured genuine turquoise for its brilliant blue color.

Materials

Mold release

Vinyl-coated wire (like telephone wire)

Liquid polymer clay

Tools

Large mold of Mayan face or similar image

Sculpting tools (optional)

Wire cutters

TURQUOISE RECIPE ON PAGE 29

Instructions

1. Chop the turquoise polymer clay mix in the food processor as described in the recipe.

2. Apply mold release to the mold, and then fill it with chopped polymer clay. Press the clay into the indentations in the mold, adding more clay to any sparsely filled spaces. Add clay until the mold is completely filled, and press firmly into place.

3. Gently remove the clay from the mold. Use sculpting tools to carefully shape or enhance any of the features of the molded piece, if desired. Bake at the manufacturer's recommended temperature for 30 to 45 minutes, depending on the thickness of the clay.

4. When the piece is cool, you'll add a hanger to the back. Cut a piece of wire appropriate to the size of your wall hanging, and curl the ends into short spirals. (This will keep them from pulling out of the clay.) Roll two pieces of turquoise polymer clay into balls the size of marbles, and flatten them slightly with your hands. Dip the ends of the wire into the liquid clay and slightly embed each end into one of the flattened balls of clay. Press the balls firmly into place on the back of the wall hanging. Bake at the manufacturer's recommended temperature for 30 minutes.

5. When cool, continue with the recipe at step 5, adding mud and paint. Finish as directed.

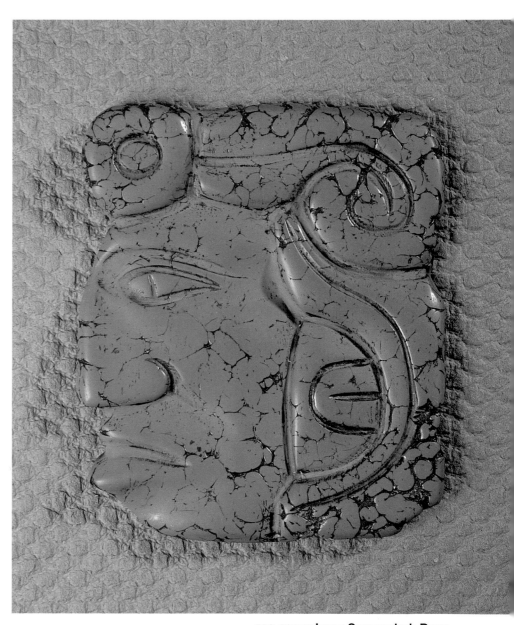

PROJECT BY **Irene Semanchuk Dean**

OPAL

Capture the shimmering iridescence of true opal using the secret ingredient, a layer of confetti suspended between translucent polymer clays.

RECIPE CONTRIBUTED BY **Irene Semanchuk Dean**

Materials

Sculpey III—Translucent

Glitter—ultra-fine iridescent and regular iridescent

Wax paper

Fimo Soft—Translucent

Confetti—iridescent

Mold release, like automobile interior protectant

Wet/dry sandpaper—400 through 1,000 grit

Polymer-friendly varnish (optional)

Tools

Cutting blade

Sculpting tool

Cabochon mold

Aluminum foil or pie pan

Buffing wheel

Instructions

1 Incorporate a small pinch of the ultra-fine glitter into a small amount of the Sculpey III translucent. Work the clay just enough to distribute the glitter through it. Roll this clay into the thinnest possible sheet, as shown, using wax paper if necessary. Set aside.

2 Use the Fimo Soft translucent to form a shape that is the size of your finished piece.

3 Cut a piece from the glittered sheet of Sculpey III that's twice as large as the top of the piece of Fimo Soft and place the glittered clay on a piece of wax paper. Place a single layer of confetti on only one half of the sheet of clay. Tear some of the confetti flakes in half if they're large, and don't overlap any of the pieces. Gently press the confetti into the surface with a sculpting tool, as shown—don't embed it, just adhere it to the surface. Sprinkle a small bit of regular-sized iridescent glitter on the same half of the sheet.

4 Carefully peel the sheet from the wax paper, using a blade to slide between the paper and the clay if necessary. Fold the clay sheet in half as shown, sandwiching the confetti and glitter, and squeeze gently to adhere completely.

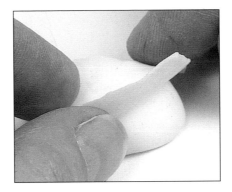

5 Lay this sheet on top of the shape you made in step 2, and press it firmly into the surface, starting in the center and working out to the edges.

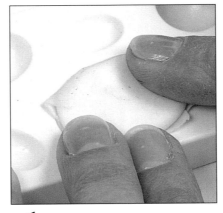

6 Apply the mold release to the cabochon mold and press the clay into the mold with the covered side down. Press very firmly—this will force adhesion between the translucent clays. Level the clay with a blade, if necessary. Remove from the mold.

7 Place your piece on a baking tray and tent with foil or cover with an inverted aluminum pie pan. Put into a cold oven, turn the heat up to the manufacturer's recommended temperature, and bake for 20 minutes. When done, turn the oven off and open the door slightly to allow the pieces to cool slowly; this will minimize plaquing.

8 Wet-sand with 400- through 1,000-grit sandpaper and buff. Add varnish if desired.

Alternative: For milky blue opal, work a small amount of pastel or light blue clay into the Fimo Soft translucent; for pinkish-red, incorporate some copper leaf at this step, and then proceed with the recipe.

earrings

These perfectly shaped opal earrings will dazzle every time, whether you're in the spotlight or in candlelight. Once you've mastered this recipe, create some matching pieces for a complete ensemble.

Materials

Rubbing alcohol

Cotton swabs

Earring backs

Cyanoacrylate glue

Tools

Small polymer clay molds (cabochon shapes)

OPAL RECIPE ON PAGE 32

Instructions

1. Form the earrings in small molds of the desired size and shape, using clay prepared according to the recipe. Bake and finish as instructed.

2. To ensure adhesion, clean the earring backs and the flat sides of the clay earrings with rubbing alcohol to eliminate any oils.

3. Use the glue to affix the backs in place.

PROJECT BY **Irene Semanchuk Dean**

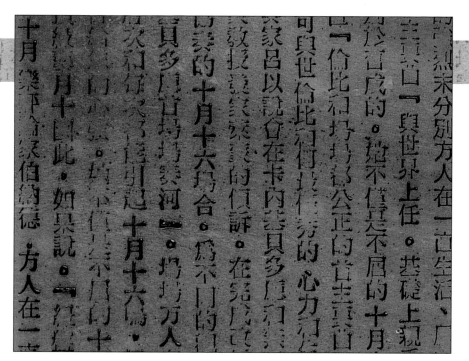

JADE

Transparent inks combine beautifully with polymer clay to simulate the translucence and depth of true jade.

RECIPE CONTRIBUTED BY **Elizabeth Campbell**

Materials

Premo!—CFC06 (Translucent 5310 with bleach)

Piñata Inks—Rainforest Green, Lime Green, Sapphire Blue, and Havana Brown

Wet/dry sandpaper—400 through 1,000 grit

Tools

Chinese newsprint stamp

Stamp pad

Buffing wheel

Instructions

1 Tint small pieces of clay with varying amounts of the inks to create four or five similar shades of pale olive green.

2 Roll each of these colors into a snake.

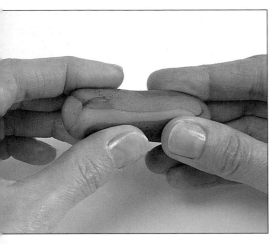

3 Next, roll, twist, and fold the snakes together to marble them. Continue to mix them until they're marbled and starting to blend, but don't blend them completely—leave some variegation.

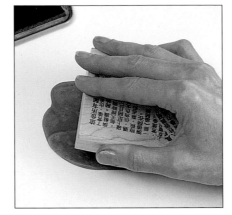

4 The clay can then be molded, stamped, or formed before baking. In this recipe, the surface is stamped with dark ink as shown, and then baked according to the manufacturer's instructions. Depending upon your chosen project, the clay can also be carved after baking.

5 Thoroughly sand the clay with 400- through 800- or 1,000-grit wet/dry sandpaper, and then buff.

Alternative: After baking (and optional carving), you can also enhance the texture of any molding or carving by rubbing burnt sienna acrylic paint onto the baked clay. Wipe off any excess with a paper towel, and allow to dry completely before sanding and buffing.

decorated pendant

Achieve the look of a precious jade artifact in this clever pendant with a hidden drawer. Embellish with coins or wire to add an ancient feel.

Materials

Aluminum foil

Permanent pigment ink—dark color

Tracing paper

Cyanoacrylate glue

Chinese coin charms—1 without loop, 3 with loop

Translucent liquid polymer clay

Brass wire, 18- and 24-gauge

Brass eye pins

1 yard (.9 m) of 2 mm nylon cord—black

Clasp (optional)

Tools

Small wooden tablet forms (from the craft store)

2 button molds

Stamps or texture sheets

Pasta machine

Chinese newsprint stamp

Cutting blade

Knitting needle

Pin vise, with bits to match sizes of your wire

Jig (optional)

Round-nose pliers

Needle-nose pliers

Side cutters

JADE RECIPE ON PAGE 35

Instructions

1. Cover your wooden tablet form with aluminum foil and smooth it tightly against the form.

2. To make the drawer, roll a piece of jade clay in the pasta machine on the third-thickest setting. It will need to be big enough to cover the bottom, back, and sides of your form. Fold the clay up against the sides of the form and meld the seams well at the corners. (The front of the drawer will be constructed in step 8.) Trim the open sides flush with the edges of the form.

3. Make three small accent beads by pressing clay between two button molds; you could also use stamps or pieces of texturing material. Ink the appropriate mold or tool before you press the beads. Bake the beads and the drawer for 15 minutes at 275°F (136°C). Set the beads aside.

4. To make the cover, leave the drawer on the form. When it's cool, wrap the form and the baked clay drawer with a single thickness of tracing paper, gluing the overlap with a drop of cyanoacrylate glue. Roll out a strip of jade clay on the first or second-thickest setting on

PROJECT BY **Elizabeth Campbell**

your pasta machine, just short of ⅛ inch (3 mm) thick. The strip will need to be long enough to go around your form once, and be as wide as the form. Stamp the strip with the inked newsprint stamp.

5. Wrap the stamped strip around the paper-covered drawer. Butt the edges together at the back and blend the seam.

6. Press a coin into the front of the strip to mark its intended location.

7. Trim the top and bottom of the strip flush with the ends of the form. Bake for 20 minutes at 275°F (136°C). When cool, remove the coin, slide the newly created cover off the drawer and form, and remove the paper.

8. Stand the open end of the drawer on a sheet of faux jade and press it into the clay slightly to mark the position. Apply a thin bead of liquid clay to the line left on the unbaked clay and place the open end of the drawer on this line. Replace the cover over the drawer, and slide it down so it's almost touching the raw clay. Cut straight down through the clay using the outside surface of the cover as a guide. Peel away

the excess clay and bake again for 15 minutes, this time boosting the temperature to 300°F (150°C) for the last five minutes. To insure the proper fit, be sure to leave the cover on the drawer during this baking, but it should be slightly ajar so the two pieces don't bake together.

9. When cool, sand and buff both pieces per the surface instructions.

10. To make a bail for the pendant, wrap the 18-gauge wire closely around the knitting needle, forming a tube that's not quite as long as the drawer is wide. Snip off all but about ¼ inch (6 mm) of wire at each end of the tube, then bend the excess wire straight down. Use the pin vise to drill two holes in the top of the drawer, place a drop of glue on each wire, and push the ends of the wire into the holes. When the glue is dry, snip off the excess wire that remains inside the drawer or bend the ends into tiny loops.

11. Using the jig or the pliers, make a curled frame out of the 18-gauge wire to hang the beads and coin charms. Leave about ³⁄₁₆ inch (5 mm) of straight wire at each end to insert into the drawer

as you did for the wire tube in the previous step. Drill two holes in the bottom of the drawer to accommodate the wire frame. Add glue, insert the frame, and finish as in step 10.

12. Drill holes in the three accent beads. Create dangles from eye-pins, using the Chinese coins with loops and the three jade beads. Clip the wire close to the jade beads and create eyes at the ends to attach them to the wire frame.

13. Take a short length of the finer wire and make a decorative knot through the top of the opening in the remaining coin; take another short length of wire and make a knot through the bottom of the opening. Glue the coin to the front surface of the cover. Drill tiny holes in the front of the cover, put a small drop of glue on the ends of the wires, and insert them into the holes. Pull the wire through and trim the excess with side cutters. Slide the cover over the drawer and string the nylon cord through the coiled wire bail. To finish the cord, use adjustable knots or add a clasp, if desired.

Alternative: Make box pendant forms from matchboxes, too.

II
Metals

BALINESE SILVER

The distinctive swirls, twists, and coils of Balinese silver can be re-created with the help of a simple clay extruder.

RECIPE CONTRIBUTED BY **Diane Villano**

Materials

Strong polymer clay—black

Mica powder—silver

Cotton swab

Polymer-friendly varnish

Tools

Pasta machine or roller

Polymer clay blade

Clay gun

Brushes

Instructions

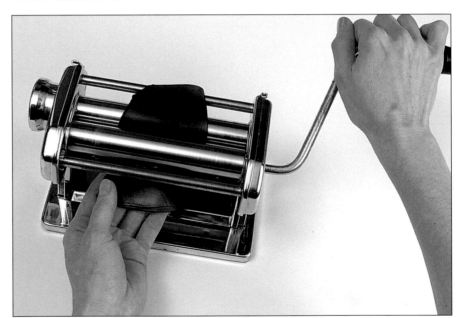

1 Roll out a medium-thin sheet of conditioned black clay.

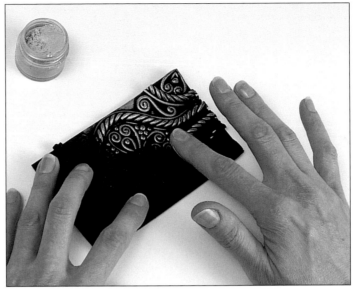

2 Load your clay gun with very well-conditioned black clay. Fit one of the round dies into the clay gun, and experiment until you find the size you feel looks best for your form. Extrude the clay into short lengths as shown and form them into swirls, scrolls, or anything that appeals to you. (Extruded clay seems to lose its conditioning fairly quickly, so try to form the lengths the same day you extruded them. If the lengths crack when you form them, simply recondition the clay and extrude again.) Gently press them onto the clay in your desired pattern. If you like, apply additional small balls of clay to your design.

3 With your finger or a cotton swab, apply the silver mica powder to your design, highlighting only the raised areas; some of the powder will migrate to the background and color it.

4 Bake the clay according to the manufacturer's instructions and let cool. Brush off any excess mica powder. Apply a thin coat of varnish to protect the mica powder, and let dry.

finial

This versatile finial can be used on a lamp, a curtain rod, or a drapery tieback. The gleaming faux silver finish imparts an elegance that surpasses mere hardware.

Materials

Wooden form

Heat-resistant PVA white glue

Tools

Drill and bit in the appropriate size for your project

Paintbrush

Craft knife or cutting blade

BALINESE SILVER RECIPE ON PAGE 40

PROJECT BY **Diane Villano**

Instructions

1. Bake the wooden form for 30 minutes at 275°F (136°C) to eliminate excess moisture and reduce the chance of cracking. When the wood is cool, drill a hole in the bottom that is the appropriate size for your hardware. Coat the form with a thin layer of white glue and let dry.

2. Roll out a medium-thin sheet of conditioned black clay, as instructed in the recipe. Cut a strip from the sheet the same width as the length of your wooden form, and long enough to go completely around it. Roll the clay strip around the form, being very careful not to trap air pockets between the form and the clay. Working from the widest part of the form, gradually press the clay to the form and work your way toward the ends. Trim the excess clay and smooth the seam by pressing with your finger or rolling the form gently on your work surface.

3. Apply the decorative elements and mica powder as described in the recipe, and bake and finish as directed.

BRONZE

This wonderfully simple process, utilizing very few ingredients, produces the rich luster of true bronze.

RECIPE CONTRIBUTED BY **Dawn Schiller**

Materials

Premo!—Burnt Umber and Copper

Mica powder—gold

Tools

Pasta machine

Paintbrush

Alternative: Different brands of gold mica powder will produce variations in color, so you might experiment if you prefer a more tarnished look, for instance.

Instructions

1 Thoroughly mix the two colors together, using 8 parts burnt umber + 1 part copper.

2 After the clay is formed or sculpted into the desired shape, randomly brush with the gold mica powder, covering most of the clay surface. If you plan to use a mold, brush it with the mica powder also. Bake at 275°F (136°C) for 30 minutes.

TIP: If your faux bronze piece will be handled frequently, use a polymer-friendly varnish to prevent the mica powder from rubbing off.

green man wall hanging

The versatility of polymer clay enables you to create this fluid sculpture. Use an actual leaf to fashion this evocative work.

Materials

Large natural leaf (or leaf pattern)

Paper

Craft wire

Liquid polymer clay

Cyanoacrylate glue

Tools

Pencil

Craft knife or cutting blade

Needle tool

Sculpting tools

Pasta machine

BRONZE RECIPE ON PAGE 43

TIP: A mirror comes in handy when you're sculpting a face!

Instructions

1. Choose a leaf (sycamore was used here) to be the pattern for the sculpture, or draw your own shape. Trace the leaf or other design onto a piece of paper; save the actual leaf if you want to duplicate the vein pattern.

2. Cut the leaf shape from the sheet of bronze clay, using the paper template as a guide. To make the stem, cut a slit along the length of a snake of bronze clay and insert the wire. Smooth the seam with your fingers; shape the stem as desired and attach. Use the needle tool to poke two holes in the back of the clay leaf, toward the stem end, to accommodate a wire from which the finished piece will hang.

3. Use a needle tool to mark the vein pattern into the clay leaf. Turn up or turn under the edges of the lobes on the leaf to give a sense of movement and dimension.

4. Decide on the placement of the features; it's usually easiest to start with the eyes. Sculpt the eyes by rolling two balls of clay to the desired size and pressing into position on the face. Make a crescent moon-shaped depression in each eye. To make the eyelids, roll a piece of clay to span the top of the eye, flatten slightly, and press into place. Smooth the seams with a finger or a sculpting tool. Repeat for the lower lid. For a different look, use iridescent marbles for the eyes.

5. Brush the clay lightly with gold mica powder per the recipe; some of the clay color should show through the powder. Bake according to the manufacturer's instructions.

6. When the sculpture is cool, make a mark for the placement of the nose. Divide in half the space between this mark and the bottom of the leaf; make a mark in this area for the placement of the mouth.

7. Using more of the bronze clay, sculpt the nose and mouth. If the clay doesn't stick well to the baked leaf, use a couple of drops of liquid polymer clay to help it stay in place.

For the nose, roll a ball of clay into a teardrop shape and flatten one side. Place the flattened side on the face. Smooth the sides and bottom seam, and use the sculpting tool to make nostrils.

For the upper lip, make a wedge of clay that's thicker in the middle and bottom; place it under the nose and blend into the face. Sculpt the line that runs under the nose by indenting a groove in the middle where the clay is thicker. Shape the bottom portion of the wedge into the upper lip.

For the lower lip, use a smaller wedge with the thicker portion on the top; blend into the face. Make a small line to indicate the corners of the mouth where the lips meet.

8. Brush the new features lightly with the gold mica powder, allowing some of the bronze color to remain. Bake according to the manufacturer's directions.

9. Roll some more bronze clay through the pasta machine on the second thickest setting; cut out a partial leaf shape using the top part of the template. Sculpt this partial leaf around the eyes and on the cheeks, again striving for a sense of movement. Smooth the edges with your finger or a sculpting tool.

10. Brush the partial leaf shapes lightly with the mica powder as before. Bake according to the manufacturer's directions.

11. Use the glue to fix both ends of a short wire into the holes in the back of the piece. Hang as desired.

PROJECT BY **Dawn Schiller**

RUSTED STEEL

Reproduce the gritty look of aged, rusted steel by adding particles of baked clay to a sheet of raw clay.

RECIPE CONTRIBUTED BY **Alison Ingham**

Materials

Premo!—Gold, Raw Sienna, Burnt Umber, Black, Silver

Wet/dry sandpaper—1,000 grit

Acrylic paint—burnt umber

Water

Polymer-friendly varnish—matte

Tools

Pasta machine

Smoothing tool, like a paint pusher or paintbrush handle

Small food grater, like a nutmeg grater

Small containers

Sculpting tool or small spoon

Artist's paintbrush cover or drinking straw (optional)

Screwdriver (optional)

Scalpel

Paintbrush

Instructions

1 First, you'll make five different clay mixes. For the rust mixtures, use small amounts in the proportions that follow: 1 part gold + 2 parts raw sienna; 1 part gold + 2 parts burnt umber; 1 part gold + 1 part black + 1 part burnt umber; and a small amount of burnt umber only.

For the background steel, make a larger amount of mix from 3 parts silver + 1 part black.

2 Divide the rust mixes in half, and bake one half of each color for 20 to 30 minutes at 275°F (136°C). Leave the clay you're baking in lumps, as you'll be grating it in a later step.

3 Roll the steel mixture through the pasta machine on the thickest setting about 15 times to align the mica particles. Scrunch the sheet into a ball, being careful to avoid creating air bubbles, roll smooth in your palms, and flatten slightly.

4 Take a small piece of the unbaked gold + burnt umber mix, and roll through the pasta machine on the thinnest setting. Tear pieces from this sheet, arranging them in a random way on one side of the steel mixture, as shown. Smooth the edges of the "rust" patches to blend the colors, using the tool of your choice.

5 Roll the steel mixture through the pasta machine on the thickest setting. Continue until the desired thickness of the finished sheet is reached. Trim the sheet to the appropriate shape.

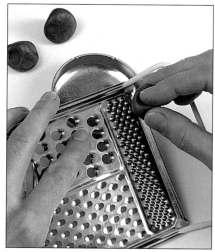

6 Take the baked piece of gold + raw sienna, and grate it into a small container using the nutmeg grater. Repeat for each rust mixture, keeping the colors separate. Make a note to identify each color, as they will look lighter once grated.

7 Starting with the gold + raw sienna mix, apply the particles to the rust patches on the sheet you made in step 5. A small tool or spoon helps, as you see in the photo. Press down the particles with your fingertips. Continue adding the other colors of grated clay in this fashion, putting small areas of one color next to the previous one. Don't go all the way to the edge of the rust patches, because this application suggests the metal is slowly rusting.

8 If you wish, you can imitate screws to enhance the metallic effect. Using a drinking straw or paintbrush cover, press small circles in the clay sheet. To make the head of the screw, press the tip of a screwdriver into the center of each circle, as shown, and add tiny marks with a scalpel between the four points of the screwdriver imprint.

9 Bake the sheet at 275°F (136°C) for 30 to 40 minutes.

10 Once cool, sand using only 1,000-grit wet/dry sandpaper. Be gentle, as you want to retain as much of the texture as possible; sand only to remove any loose particles and dull any sharp pieces.

11 Mix up a thin wash of burnt umber acrylic paint and water (more water than paint), and brush over the rust particles, as shown. The paint will pool around the bottom of each particle. While still wet, add patches of wash in a denser color, which will spread out and also pool.

12 When dry, coat with polymer-friendly matte varnish.

picture frame

Tigger looks positively beguiling as she peers from this unique frame of faux rusted steel. Simulated screws contribute to the convincing effect of this imitative surface.

Materials

Wooden picture frame

Heat-resistant PVA white glue

Polymer clay—scrap pieces

Tools

Cutting blade

Pin

RUSTED STEEL RECIPE ON PAGE 46

Instructions

1. Remove the glass and backing board from the frame and set aside.

2. Cover the frame with a thin coating of glue. Let it sit for a few moments so it's almost dry, but still tacky.

3. Make a sheet of the faux surface that's large enough to cover the entire frame, but don't yet add the grated clay.

4. Trim the sheet to the appropriate size for your frame. First cover the sides to the right and left of the picture opening, including their outer edges. Prick out any air bubbles, and smooth the edges at the back of the frame with your finger.

5. Before you cover the bare frame that remains above and below the picture opening, first add a layer of scrap clay. Use clay that's the same thickness as the sheets already in place on the frame, so the entire front is level—you'll cover this scrap clay in the next step, as well as the remaining edges.

6. Trim pieces of the faux sheet that are long enough to cover the scrap clay you just placed above and below the picture opening, including the remaining side edges. Place these pieces on the frame, and smooth over as before. The top and bottom should now be elevated above the level of the sides.

7. Add the imitation screws as directed in the rusted steel recipe.

8. Add the grated clay to the frame, per the surface recipe. Bake the frame for about 45 minutes at the manufacturer's recommended temperature.

9. After the frame is cool, follow the recipe to complete the rust effect: sand; add the paint wash; and varnish.

10. Replace the glass, add a favorite picture, and insert the backing board.

PROJECT BY **Alison Ingham**

PEWTER

The traditional look of
pewter, which has been used
for utensils and tableware
for centuries, is updated
here with whimsical stamps.

RECIPE CONTRIBUTED BY **Heather Roselli**

Materials

Strong polymer clay—black

Rub 'n Buff—Silver Leaf

Cotton swab

Soft cloth

Polymer-friendly varnish—satin

Tools

**Texturing tools, like stamps,
    cutters, molds, or sheets**

Paintbrush

Instructions

1 After conditioning, stamp
    images or symbols into the
black clay; you could also use
any kind of textured object to
embellish the clay. Leave slight
fingerprint and other imperfections in the surface to create a
distressed or aged appearance.

2 Bake according to the
    manufacturer's instruc-
tions. Let cool.

3 Dab a tiny amount of the
    silver wax compound on a
cotton swab or your fingertip.
Wipe the excess across a paper
towel, and then rub the cooled
clay object with a fairly dry swab
or finger, applying color only to
raised areas, not the impressed
surfaces. Allow the wax compound to set for about 15 minutes. Buff lightly with soft cloth.

4 Coat the surface with a
    polymer-friendly varnish.
Then, bake for another 10 minutes to set the finish.

Alternative: For a different look,
attach raised objects that are
sculpted, molded, or cut from
black clay.

wine stoppers

These distinctive stoppers will add an elegant finishing touch to your next dinner party. Create a simple covered stopper, or add some decorative elements for an extra flourish.

Materials

Wine bottle stoppers (from a kitchen supply catalog)

Premo!—Black

Translucent liquid polymer clay

Sheet of card stock

Tools

Pasta machine

Cutting blade

Small terra cotta flower pot

PEWTER RECIPE ON PAGE 50

Instructions

(for the stopper at right, below)

1. Unscrew the top of the stopper from the bottom section.

PROJECT BY **Heather Roselli**

wine stoppers

2. Cover the top of the stopper with a sheet of black clay rolled to the thickest setting on your pasta machine. Cut the bottom edge flush with the stopper. Stamp as directed in the surface recipe.

3. To make a decorative top element for the stopper, roll a ball of clay approximately 1½ inches (3.8 cm) in diameter. Form a bicone shape, then cut away the bottom point to flatten. Apply liquid clay to the flattened bottom and press it onto the top of the covered bottle stopper. Use the stamps as specified in the recipe instructions to embellish the top of the stopper.

4. Turn the small pot upside down, place the threaded end of the bottle stopper into the hole in the pot, and bake at 275°F (136°C) for 30 minutes. Turn the oven off and allow to cool slowly.

5. Apply the wax compound and finish as directed in the surface instructions.

6. Reassemble the wine stopper.

(for the stopper at left, page 51)

1. Unscrew the top of the stopper from the bottom section; the top of this stopper has a flat chrome edge on the bottom.

2. Cover the top of the stopper with a sheet of black clay rolled to the thickest setting of your pasta machine. Taper the edge of the clay at the bottom of the stopper, and cut the bottom edge of the clay flush with the stopper. Stamp as directed in the surface recipe.

3. Bake the covered top of the stopper chrome side down on card stock at 275°F (136°C) for 30 minutes. Turn off the oven to cool slowly.

4. Apply the wax compound and finish as directed in the surface instructions.

5. Reassemble the wine stopper.

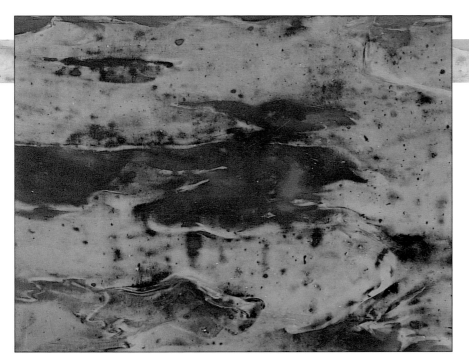

COPPER VERDIGRIS

Random distressing and careful layering result in a surface that's difficult to distinguish from true antique copper.

RECIPE CONTRIBUTED BY **Alison Ingham**

Materials

Premo!—Burnt Umber, Gold, Copper, Black, Sea Green, Alizarin Crimson, Cadmium Yellow, and White

Acrylic paint—burnt umber

Talcum powder or cornstarch (optional)

Polymer-friendly varnish—matte

Wet/dry sandpaper—1,000 grit (optional)

Tools

Pasta machine

Tools for punching (like a stylus) and smoothing (like a paint pusher)

Cutting blade

Rolling pin, acrylic rod, or brayer

Mold (optional)

Paintbrush

Instructions

1 Start by mixing several colors. First, create a base color by thoroughly mixing 2 parts burnt umber + 1 part gold + 1 part copper.

Make a small amount of dark copper by mixing a bit of the mixed base color with twice that amount of black.

Lastly, make a verdigris color by thoroughly mixing 4 parts sea green + 1 part alizarin crimson + 1 part cadmium yellow + 14 parts white. (Adjust the colors if you want to make the verdigris lighter or darker.) You'll also need a small amount of black equal to the amount of the verdigris mixture.

2 Roll the base sheet mixture to medium thickness on the pasta machine. (If you want to make a project that will result in the copper verdigris being used as a flat sheet, cut off about a quarter of the sheet and set to one side. See the detailed instructions on page 55.)

3 Roll the dark copper mixture to the thinnest possible setting on a pasta machine. Lay the thin sheet on a smooth work surface, and use a blunt tool to make random holes in the sheet and along the edges, as shown. Use the blade to carefully remove the sheet from the work surface.

4 Place the base sheet from step 2 on a smooth work surface. Start in one corner and place the dark copper sheet on top of the base sheet, stretching it gently as you press it down.

5 Using a smoothing tool, blend the edges of the dark copper sheet into the base sheet as shown. Use a rolling pin or brayer to smooth the surface. Set to one side.

6 Roll out the black clay to the thinnest setting on the pasta machine and place on a smooth work surface. Roll out the verdigris mix to the thinnest setting on the pasta machine, and lay this sheet on top of the black sheet. Roll the sheet thinner using a rolling pin, and trim so you can't see any black clay. Use a blunt tool to make random holes in this sheet and around the edges as in step 3. Carefully remove from your work surface with the blade.

7 Place the verdigris sheet, green side up, onto one corner of the base sheet with the dark copper overlay you made in step 5. Stretch the verdigris sheet gently as you press it down, just as you did in step 4. It may tear since it's very thin, creating patches of verdigris. You can add more pieces of this sheet as you wish, but try not to overlap the verdigris sheet as you apply it.

8 Use a smoothing tool to blend the edges of the verdigris sheet into the main sheet, as in step 5. Use a rolling pin to smooth the surface.

9 Roll the sheet through the pasta machine at a medium setting. Roll through progressively thinner settings on the pasta machine, stopping when the verdigris color begins to blend and look thinner.

To use in a mold:

1 Prepare your mold by dusting it with talcum powder or cornstarch as a release agent. Lay the sheet, verdigris side down, over the mold, as shown; use some scrap clay to fill in the mold, if necessary. This thins the verdigris even more, enhancing the look. Remove from the mold and trim the excess clay.

2 Bake the molded piece as recommended by the manufacturer. Once cool, apply a thin wash of burnt umber acrylic paint, just enough to let it collect in the grooves, and let dry. The wash gives the verdigris a slightly greener look and enhances the details of a molded piece. Once dry, apply polymer-friendly matte varnish if desired.

To use as a flat sheet:

1 Roll out a sheet of base color mix (which was set aside in step 2 on page 54) to medium thickness, and lay the verdigris copper sheet onto this sheet, verdigris side up. Continue rolling this sheet through the pasta machine one or two steps thinner, or until you like the patina. Don't roll the sheet too thin or the verdigris will become too pale to be effective.

2 Bake the sheet as recommended by the manufacturer.

3 To enhance the look of a flat baked piece, sand the surface with 1,000-grit wet/dry sandpaper. This removes some areas of the patina to create a mottled effect. Since real copper verdigris has a matte finish, either leave the surface as it is, or varnish it with polymer-friendly matte varnish.

fish napkin rings

In Chinese tradition, the fish symbolizes abundance and togetherness. Bring these qualities to your next gathering with these molded napkin rings.

Materials

Fine-gauge craft wire

Polymer clay—scrap pieces

Talcum powder

Mold of your choice

Paper towel tube

Wet/dry sandpaper—1,000 grit (optional)

Tools

Small, oven-safe glass bottle or jar, approximately 2 inches (5 cm) wide

Scalpel

COPPER VERDIGRIS RECIPE ON PAGE 53

Instructions

1. Wrap a piece of wire around the bottle five or six times and twist the ends together; this will be the base for the napkin ring. Check that you can remove the coil of wire later by sliding it to the bottom of the jar, or you will have to smash the glass! Adjust the tightness of the wire if necessary.

2. Using scrap clay, make several test pieces from your chosen mold to see how many molded pieces you'll need to make a complete ring. (In this project, each ring is composed of two molded fish.) Place the test pieces around the coil, and examine how well they fit together.

3. Once you're happy with the design, make the necessary number of molded pieces from a sheet of faux copper verdigris. Gently lay these pieces over the wire coil in the same pattern as your test pieces. Don't press too hard or you will obliterate the details of your molded pieces, but be sure the pieces stick to the glass bottle, too. Once you are happy with the arrangement, bake the ring on the bottle for 30 minutes at the manufacturer's recommended temperature.

4. When cool, remove the ring by carefully sliding the scalpel around the inside of the ring.

5. Decide on a color for the inside of the ring; these are dark copper. Roll your chosen clay to a medium setting on your pasta machine. Then, with talcum powder on your fingertips, press the strips over the wire inside the ring. Since this step is a bit tricky, start from one end of each strip and work your way along.

6. Once the inside is covered and smooth, use the scalpel to trim off the excess clay. Apply more powder to your fingertip and smooth the unbaked clay to the inside of the napkin ring.

7. Bake again for 30 minutes, placing the napkin rings on a paper towel tube for support during baking.

8. When the rings are cool, remove the support and wet-sand the edges if necessary, using 1,000-grit wet/dry paper.

9. Apply the paint wash and finish as indicated in the recipe.

PROJECT BY **Alison Ingham**

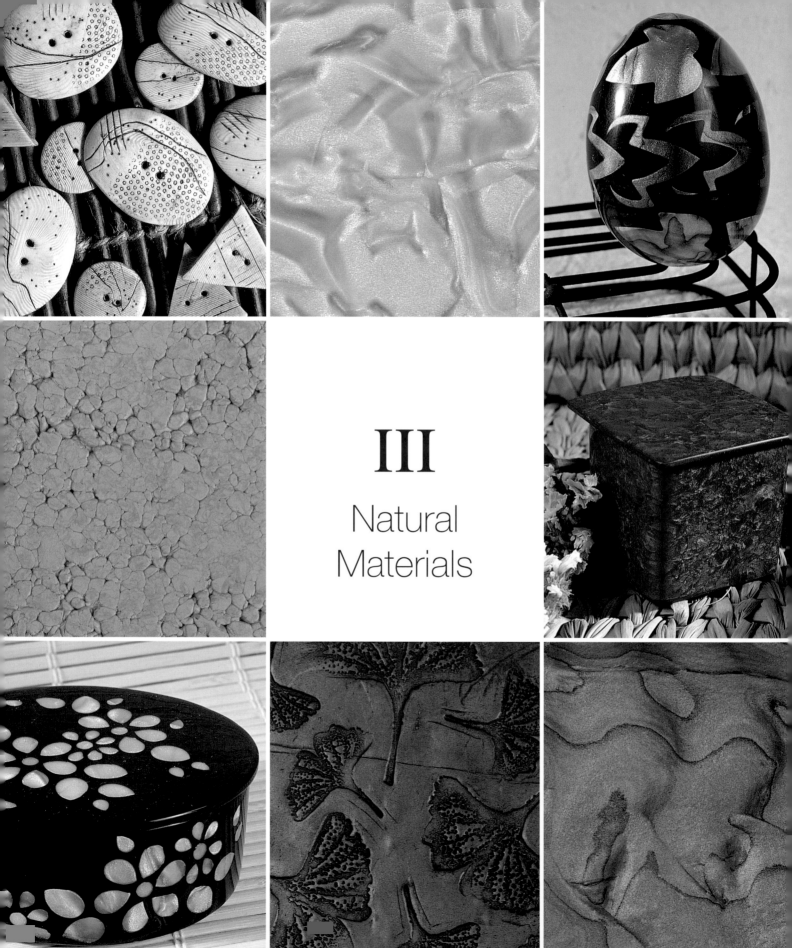

III

Natural
Materials

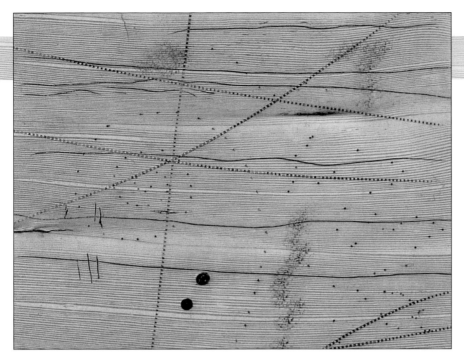

BONE

Ultra-fine layers of differently colored clay resemble the fine graining of real bone and ivory; folding, stretching, and refolding quickly translates into hundreds of extremely fine layers.

RECIPE CONTRIBUTED BY **Luann Udell**

Materials

Polymer clay—beige, white, gold, and translucent

Wet/dry sanding sponges— fine, superfine and ultra-fine grits (or the equivalent wet/dry sandpaper)

Acrylic paint in your choice of "dirt" colors—raw umber, burnt umber, black, dark brown, etc.

Paper towel or rag

Tools

Pasta machine

Cutting blade

Rolling pin or acrylic rod

Texturing tools, like a stylus, pins, sewing needles, screws, or similar objects

Linoleum block cutter (optional)

Buffing wheel

Instructions

1 Thoroughly mix equal amounts of the beige and white clays to create an ivory shade; then add a small bit of gold for an aged bone appearance, if desired. Roll it into a sheet using the thickest setting on your pasta machine.

2 Roll the translucent clay into a sheet the same thickness as the "bone" clay. Lay the bone sheet on top of the translucent sheet and trim the edges to make a rectangle.

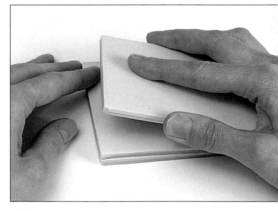

3 Cut your rectangle into thirds and stack as shown. Trim any layers that overlap significantly.

4 Use the rolling pin or acrylic rod to gently but firmly roll the stack of clay. Turn the stack so you stretch it equally in all directions, and use your fingers to gently stretch the stack so it maintains a square or rectangular form. Make sure the stack stays a uniform thickness throughout. When the stack is stretched large enough to cut in half again, do so with your cutting blade, as shown.

5 Stack these two layers and gently manipulate them so all the edges align as much as possible. Trim, roll, and stretch this stack as in steps 3 and 4.

6 As you trim, examine the cross-section of layers. When they are as thin as you want but still clearly visible, stop the process. If you continue too far, the graining will become too fine for the eye to discern. Slice off cross-sections of faux bone to use in your projects.

7 If desired, you can cut artifacts directly from the slices, keeping the grain of the bone intact.

8 To create patterns and designs in your piece, mark the clay with your texturing tools, as shown, and bake. Or, you can bake the object and then carve with a linoleum block cutter when the clay has cooled. If necessary, wet-sand with the sponges or sandpaper.

9 Use your fingers to apply a coating of the dark acrylic paint to the baked clay, being sure to work it into the crevices of the markings. Wipe off the excess paint with a paper towel or rag, as shown, and buff the finished surface when the paint has dried.

TIP: For a whiter ivory, reduce the amount of beige and increase the amount of white, or use equal amounts of white and translucent mixed together instead. If you use a soft clay, which gets mushy quickly when handled, you can let the finished block leach overnight.

buttons

These buttons—remarkably similar to ancient bone—will really make a personal statement on a special garment. The properties of polymer clay allow you to make the buttons any size or shape you desire.

Materials

Polymer clay—beige

Tools

Plastic wrap or parchment paper

Acrylic roller or brayer

Knitting needle or similar tool

BONE RECIPE ON PAGE 59

Instructions

1. Roll marble-sized balls of beige clay. Cover these with thin slices of faux bone. Roll in your cupped hands to smooth the surface.

2. Gently flatten each ball. To do this evenly, first roll the ball of clay into your preferred shape (round, oval, etc.), set it on your work surface, and press with your fingers to flatten slightly. Place a piece of plastic wrap or parchment paper on each button, and flatten more with a roller or brayer.

3. Use a knitting needle, pencil point, or other pointed tool to make two holes in each button. Flip over the buttons to make sure the holes go completely through, and smooth the clay around the exit holes.

4. Add texture to the surface of the buttons and finish per the bone recipe. To cut down or even eliminate sanding, place the buttons on your baking surface, lay a piece of plastic wrap or parchment paper on top of each button and gently stroke the surface to smooth it. Stroke with enough pressure to eliminate fingerprints, but not so much that you obliterate your texturing.

5. Bake and finish per the surface recipe. Use these buttons only on hand-washable items, as they can't withstand the heat of the dryer.

PROJECT BY **Luann Udell**

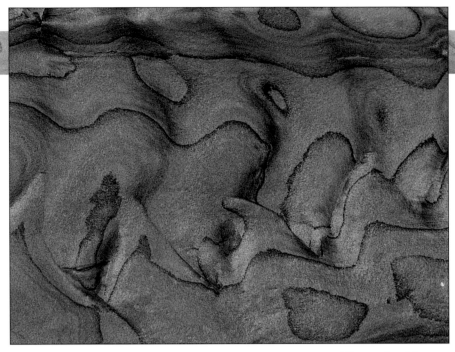

ABALONE

Since abalone can reflect many colors of the spectrum, use several metallic colors of polymer clay to imitate nature at its most brilliant.

RECIPE CONTRIBUTED BY **Chryse Laukkonen**

Materials

Premo!—Pearl and Black, plus several colors of your choosing, like Blue Pearl, Green Pearl, Gold, and Purple

Oil paint—black

Wet/dry sandpaper—400 through 800 grit

Polymer-friendly varnish (optional)

Tools

Cutting blade

Brayer or pasta machine

Paintbrush handle (optional)

Ripple blade (optional)

Buffing wheel

Instructions

1 Begin with the pearl clay and mix in a little black clay to create a nice silver. Add small pinches of black to the pearl until it's a shade you like. The mix used for this surface is about 1 part pearl + $\frac{1}{32}$ part black.

2 Divide the silver mixture into sections equal to the number of colors you plan to use. Leave one section silver, but tint the others by mixing in small pinches from each of your chosen colors.

3 Roll out the color mixtures into sheets of varying thickness using the brayer or pasta machine; make sheets about $\frac{1}{32}$ to $\frac{1}{16}$ inch (.8 mm to 1.6 mm) thick. Varying the thickness of these sheets helps produce the genuine abalone look in the final surface.

4 Cut or tear pieces out of the sheets of clay that are about 2 by 3 inches (5 x 7.6 cm). (If you'd rather tear the sheets, and the clay wants to stretch rather than tear, let it cool down; toss it into the freezer for about 10 minutes if necessary.) Set aside one piece (any color) to use in step 6. Then, randomly stack anywhere from two to five differently colored squares to create a number of small stacks, as shown. It's okay to occasionally repeat the same color, as it will just make a broader band of color in the abalone.

5 Smear a very, very small amount of the black oil paint on top of each stack. Don't paint the sheet you set aside in the previous step.

6 Now, layer the painted stacks on top of each other; place the unpainted sheet on top of these. Press from the top to adhere the sheets to one another. Make indentations by poking your fingers or knuckles (or a tool like a paintbrush handle) in from the top and bottom of the stack, as shown.

7 Let the stack rest and cool before slicing across the top in mokume gane style. Try slicing with a regular blade and with a ripple blade to see which gives the most realistic effect.

8 You can run the slices or sheet through the pasta machine again, if desired—this produces muted segments of color in the final surface. (To use as an inlay, apply the slices from the abalone stack to a background piece of clay and cut into the desired shapes. See the project instructions on page 64 for more information.) Bake according to the manufacturer's directions. Wet-sand, buff, and varnish the final project as desired.

mosaic egg

Mother Nature couldn't make eggs this beautiful, but you can! Cut shapes from a sheet of faux abalone clay and create a veneer that features stunning color play. A bowl of these eggs will make an unforgettable centerpiece.

Materials

Blown natural egg, wooden egg, or plastic egg

Translucent liquid polymer clay or heat-resistant PVA white glue

Polymer clay—black

Tools

Cutting blade

Shape cutters (optional)

ABALONE RECIPE ON PAGE 62

Instructions

1. Prepare the egg by applying a base coat of liquid clay or glue.

2. Cut slices from the abalone stack and make a sheet of clay by either adhering together at the edges or applying them to the top of a sheet of scrap clay, creating a veneer sheet. Roll through the pasta machine to a medium thickness.

3. Using cutters or freehand, cut out shapes from the sheet and apply them to the egg, leaving some space in between the pieces. Bake according to the manufacturer's instructions.

4. Allow the item to cool and then backfill with another color; black complements this faux abalone well. Simply press the clay between the shapes and smooth. Bake again according to the manufacturer's instructions.

5. Allow the egg to cool. Sand and finish as described in the surface directions.

> **TIP:** If you use a plastic egg, slice it open after the first baking and remove the melted plastic.

PROJECT BY **Chryse Laukkonen**

CORK

This technique uses chopped metallic polymer clay to imitate the characteristic texture of cork.

RECIPE CONTRIBUTED BY **Irene Semanchuk Dean**

Materials

Premo!—Gold and Ecru

Wax paper

Wet/dry sandpaper—400 and 600 grit

Tools

Food processor

Sheet of clear acrylic

Brayer or acrylic rod

Pasta machine

Instructions

1 Mix 3 parts gold + 2 parts ecru. Roll the clay mixture into a sheet and place between two pieces of white paper to leach (see page 14). Allow it to leach for at least several hours; overnight is okay, too. The paper will absorb some of the plasticizer in the clay, which will make it chop more finely in the next step.

2 Tear the sheet of polymer clay into strips, and then tear the strips into small pieces. Toss these into the bowl of the food processor, and run it in short bursts so you're able to see the changes in the clay: it will start to form small balls, like those shown, and the more the clay has been leached, the

smaller the balls will be. Small pieces will be more effective for creating an accurate faux cork.

3 Pour the chopped polymer onto a sheet of waxed paper. Set aside a small portion of the balls to fill in the gaps later, in step 6.

4 With your hand, spread the chopped clay evenly on the wax paper. Press it gently into place, and fill in larger open areas with some of the balls from the edges.

5 Place another piece of wax paper on top of the clay, and place the acrylic sheet on top of that. Press straight down, enough to slightly flatten the clay. Remove the acrylic sheet and wax paper, then gently roll over the surface with a brayer or rod as shown; this will flatten the clay enough to go through the pasta machine in the next step. Be sure to roll in two directions, perpendicular to each other, so you don't push the clay too far in either direction and lose the effect of the flattened balls of clay.

6 Use the balls you set aside in step 3 to fill in any open spaces. Roll the sheet through the pasta machine at the thickest setting. Turn the clay 90°, set the pasta machine one notch thinner, and roll the clay through again.

7 After baking, wet-sand with 400- and 600-grit sandpaper. Don't move to higher grits or buff the clay, because you don't want this surface to shine.

switch plate

The textural interest of cork adds visual appeal to these simple switch plates, which are crafted with ease. Create many of these unique accents for your home.

Materials

Plastic or metal switch plate

Heat-resistant PVA glue

CORK RECIPE ON PAGE 65

Tools

Pasta machine

Brayer (optional)

Small circle cutter or drinking straw

Craft knife

Instructions

1. Cover the switch plate with a thin coat of glue and set aside to dry.

2. Prepare the recipe for faux cork. When you have run it through the pasta machine to a medium thickness (turning 90° after each pass), carefully place the faux cork sheet on the front of the switch plate, allowing the sides to extend beyond the edges of the underlying plate. Press gently outward from the center with your hand or a brayer, pushing any air bubbles out the side.

3. Remove the clay from the screw holes using the small circle cutter or drinking straw, and cut the clay out of the toggle hole(s) with the craft knife.

4. Bake the switch plate at the manufacturer's recommended temperature for 20 minutes.

5. Allow to cool, and sand as directed in the surface recipe.

PROJECT BY **Irene Semanchuk Dean**

MOTHER-OF-PEARL

The iridescent sheen of mother-of-pearl can be replicated with the use of very small amounts of colored mica powders; let inspiration be your guide as you choose the shades.

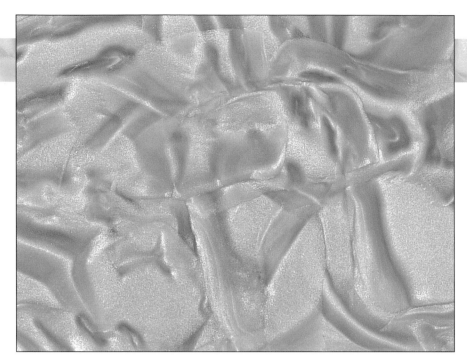

RECIPE CONTRIBUTED BY **Elizabeth Campbell**

Materials

Premo!—Pearl

Powdered Pearls—various colors such as Carnation Pink, Yellow, Turquoise, Fuchsia, and Pearl Dust

Wax paper

Wet/dry sandpaper—400 through 800 grit (optional)

Nitrile gloves (optional)

Tools

Pasta machine

Cutting blade

Brayer or acrylic rod

Distressing tools, like a paintbrush handle or credit card

Buffing wheel

Ceramic tile

Shape cutters (from a craft store)

Instructions

1 Tint a sheet of pearl clay by applying stripes of mica powders. (If you prefer a pale mother-of-pearl, with barely perceptible color, use very little mica powder.) Fold the sheet in half from bottom to top, and run through the pasta machine again, folded edge first. Repeat 10 to 20 times—as though you were making a Skinner blend—until the colors are distributed through the pearl clay as shown, leaving subtle stripes of color.

2 Cut the sheet in two, and stack one piece on the other so the colors don't line up. Put a piece of wax paper over the clay and roll over it to adhere the two sheets. Cut this sheet once lengthwise and two or three times widthwise, and stack again. Compress and stretch this stack with your hands as shown; it doesn't have to be even.

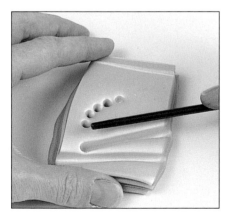

3 Cut the stack into quarters, re-stack and compress again. As shown, distress

this stack with some kind of thin tool—a paintbrush handle or a credit card bent into a "U" shape works well. (The distressing should be not be as pronounced as in mokume gane.) Compress the stack from the sides to make it taller, and let it rest.

4 Cut very thin and irregular slices from the top of the block, turn them upside down and arrange them on a piece of wax paper, as shown. Keep the pattern irregular, and cover the less-than-beautiful slices with

prettier ones. When the clay has built up to a thickness about the same as the thickest setting on your pasta machine, cover the clay with a second sheet of paper and roll over it with an acrylic rod or a brayer to stick the pieces together.

5 Remove the paper and run the clay through the thickest setting on the pasta machine, turn it a quarter turn, and run it through at the next setting. Repeat and stop at a medium thickness setting.

6 Mother-of-pearl is often used as an inlay. However, to use the entire sheet, shape the clay or cover an object and bake according to manufacturer's instructions. Allow to cool, then sand with 400- through 800-grit sandpaper and buff lightly on a cotton buffing wheel.

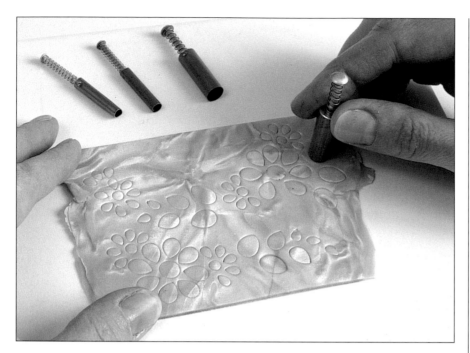

box with inlay

Let this container hold only your most cherished possessions. This exquisite box is built around an oval cookie cutter and embellished with a floral motif of imitation mother-of-pearl.

Materials

Tracing paper

Cyanoacrylate glue

Premo!—Black

Liquid polymer clay—black

Wet/dry sandpaper—320 through 800 or 1,000 grit

Tools

Oval cookie cutters, one in the desired size for the box and one that is the next size larger

Cutting blade

Round and teardrop shape cutters, in the two smallest sizes available

Ceramic tile or piece of glass

Pasta machine

Craft knife

Small acrylic roller

Tweezers

Buffing wheel

MOTHER-OF-PEARL RECIPE ON PAGE 68

7 To create shapes for inlay, place the sheet on a ceramic tile, cover with a piece of paper, and roll over it gently so it's well-adhered to the tile. Cut the desired shapes with cutters, as shown, or with a cutting blade. Peel up the excess clay and bake the shapes right on the tile. Because the shapes will be inlaid into unbaked clay and re-baked, the initial baking to harden the shapes should be no longer than 10 minutes at 275°F (136°C); longer may cause the pearl clay to yellow slightly. When the pieces are cool, you can embed them in raw clay without smearing or distorting their shapes. Bake the finished pieces with the inlaid clay according to the manufacturer's directions, or about 30 minutes at 275°F (136°C). Sand and buff as in step 6.

TIP: This artist who submitted this recipe always wears gloves when she handles pearl clays to avoid embossing her fingerprints into the mica pattern.

Instructions

1. Cut a strip from your prepared sheet of faux mother-of-pearl and apply it to one side of the smaller oval cookie cutter. Smooth the clay well onto the cutter.

2. Using both sizes of the shape cutters, cut floral designs into the mother-of-pearl sheet on one side of the cookie cutter. Bake the clay on the cookie cutter for 10 minutes at 275°F (136°C) and let cool. (Baking these design elements on the cutter will allow them to conform to the curves of your box.) Remove the strip of baked clay when cool and leave it intact—it will provide a placement guide when decorating the outside of the box.

3. Adhere the rest of your mother-of-pearl sheet to a ceramic tile or piece of glass and cut out an oval with the larger cookie cutter. Using the shape cutters again, stamp out a floral design within the oval; these shapes will be on the lid. Peel away the excess clay, leaving the design elements stuck to the tile. Bake for 10 minutes at 275°F (136°C) and allow to cool.

4. Wrap the smaller cookie cutter with a single thickness of tracing paper and glue down the overlap on the outside with a drop of cyanoacrylate glue.

5. Roll a sheet of black polymer clay on the thickest setting of the pasta machine. From this sheet, cut a strip that will cover the sides of the smaller cookie cutter. Affix the strip to the cutter and smooth together where the two edges meet. Eliminate any air bubbles.

6. Trim the clay at the bottom of the cutter flush with the cutter edge. To make the bottom of the box, set the clay-covered cutter on another sheet of black clay and cut around the outside with a craft knife. Lift the clay-covered cutter with the newly cut bottom

PROJECT BY **Elizabeth Campbell**

box with inlay

intact and use a small roller to meld the seam where the sides join the bottom of the box.

7. Bake the clay on the cookie cutter for 30 minutes 275°F (136°C). Remove the clay from the cutter while it's still warm.

8. Let the box cool, and apply a second layer of black clay. Make sure that this outer surface is smooth and free of air pockets. Remove the flower motifs from the strip of faux mother-of-pearl that was baked on the cutter. Use the strip as a placement guide while you apply the pieces to their corresponding places on the soft outer layer of black clay. When the pieces are placed correctly on the front of the box, push them firmly into the clay until they are flush with the surface of the box. Roll over the surface with a small roller to smooth the surface and eliminate some sanding later.

9. Brush the inside of the box with black liquid polymer clay, allowing it to pool in the corner between the wall and floor of the box. This reinforces the box and leaves a matte finish on the interior of the box, since it's very difficult to adequately sand and buff these surfaces. Bake for 20 minutes at 275°F (136°C), then boost the temperature to 300°F (150°C) for 10 minutes. Let cool and set aside.

10. To make the top of the box, roll out a sheet of black clay on the thickest setting of the pasta machine, cut it in half, and stack it to make a double-thick sheet. Adhere this sheet to a tile, and lightly mark using the larger oval cutter. Remove the small flower and leaf pieces from the tile you baked them on in step 3, and place them within the oval on the black clay you just marked. (Tweezers will be helpful here.) When the design is arranged to your liking, push the pieces firmly into the black clay, leaving them slightly raised from the surface. Use a roller to level and smooth the surface. Use the larger oval cookie cutter to cut out the lid. Peel away the excess clay and bake the piece for 30 minutes at 275°F (136°C).

11. Roll another sheet of black clay and use the smaller oval cutter to cut a flange for the lid. Apply a little black liquid clay to the inside of the lid and center the flange onto the inside of the lid, being careful to eliminate air bubbles and to wipe away any seepage of liquid clay. Bake for 10 minutes at 275°F (136°C), and then boost the temperature to 300°F (150°C) for another 10 minutes.

12. Sand the box and the lid—start with rough 320-grit to remove the initial imperfections. Continue through as many grades of sandpaper as you wish in preparation for buffing. After sanding, first buff the box at low speed and firm pressure, and then at high speed with just a bit of pressure.

Alternative: If you don't have a buffer, you can use two or more coats of glaze to bring out the color and sparkle in the mother-of-pearl and replicate a lacquered appearance for the box.

LEATHER

Imitate textured leather with the help of acrylic paint and hand buffing; any small flaws will only add to the realism of the surface.

RECIPE CONTRIBUTED BY **Irene Semanchuk Dean**

Materials

Polymer clay—copper

Acrylic paint—black

Paper towels

Rubbing alcohol

Tools

Items to create texture, such as rubber stamps, leather tools, or texture sheets

Soft cloth

Instructions

1 Add texture to a sheet of dark copper polymer clay, as shown, creating either an indented or a raised texture.

Observe the patterns and designs used on real leather and choose your texture accordingly.

2 Bake at 275°F (136°C) for 20 to 30 minutes.

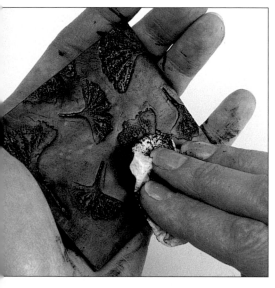

3 When cool, use your fingers to apply black acrylic paint to the texture, rubbing it into all the crevices and indentations. Remove the excess paint immediately with a paper towel, but don't rub too hard or you'll remove too much paint.

4 Allow the paint to dry for a few minutes—just about as long as it takes to wash the paint off your hands. Apply a small amount of rubbing alcohol to a paper towel and pat it over the surface of the painted clay. Rub and dab very gently to remove most of the paint from the raised areas, leaving a subtle coloration.

5 When the alcohol has evaporated, buff hard with a soft cloth to leave a sheen on the surface.

textured bowl

Store little treasures in this exquisite bowl, made from a mold of actual fern fronds. Add faux rivets for a finishing touch.

Materials

Cyanoacrylate glue

Small amount of polymer clay—silver or gold

Acrylic paint—black

Tools

Tiny circle cutter or drinking straw

Paintbrush

LEATHER RECIPE ON PAGE 73

Instructions

1. Create two sheets of faux leather with your desired texture pattern, but don't trim the edges just yet. (If you want to make a mold using fern fronds, see the directions on page 14.)

2. Place one sheet, textured side down, on your work surface; carefully place the other sheet, textured side up, on top. To begin, situate the top sheet at one edge, and with one hand, ease it onto the bottom sheet while smoothing and pressing gently into place with the other hand. If any air pockets or bubbles are visible, gently press them outward to the sides.

3. Cut this doubled, textured slab of clay into a square. Pinch the edges together at each corner so the sides of the square cup upward. Crimp gently, so you don't distort the texture. Use a small drop of cyanoacrylate glue to hold the pinched corners in place.

4. Roll the silver or gold clay into a thin sheet, and cut eight tiny circles to represent rivets holding the corners together. Set them in place, two on each corner of the bowl, opposite one another, and press to adhere.

5. Bake at the manufacturer's recommended temperature for 30 minutes.

6. When cool, follow the recipe instructions to apply paint; buff as directed to finish. Paint the rim of the bowl with black acrylic paint.

PROJECT BY **Irene Semanchuk Dean**

BURLED
RED MAPLE

The burl shown here is yet another wonderful effect produced by the mica in the metallic polymer clay used in this recipe.

RECIPE CONTRIBUTED BY **Irene Semanchuk Dean**

Materials

Premo!—Gold, Fuchsia, and Cobalt Blue

Wax paper

Wet/dry sandpaper—400 through 1,000 grit

Tools

Food processor

Piece of clear acrylic sheet

Brayer or acrylic rod

Pasta machine

Buffing wheel

Instructions

1 Mix the clay in the following ratio: 4 parts fuchsia + 3 parts gold + ½ part cobalt blue.

2 Tear or cut the polymer clay into chunks and put them in the food processor bowl. Run the machine in short bursts, until the clay has formed into small balls.

3   Dump the chopped poly-
    mer onto a sheet of wax
paper. Set aside a small portion
of the balls to fill in gaps later.

4   With your hand, spread
    the chopped clay evenly
on the waxed paper. Press it
gently into place, and fill in larger
open areas with some of the balls
from the edges.

5   Place another piece of
    waxed paper on top of the
clay, and place the acrylic sheet
on top of that. Press straight
down, enough to flatten the clay
slightly, as shown. Remove the
acrylic sheet, then gently roll over
the surface with a brayer or rod
to flatten it enough to go through
the pasta machine. Be sure to roll

in two directions, perpendicular
to each other, so you don't push
the clay too far either way and
lose the effect created by the flattened balls of clay.

6   Remove the waxed paper
    and use the balls you set
aside in step 3 to fill in any open
spaces. Roll the sheet through
the pasta machine at the thickest
setting. Turn the clay 90°, set the
pasta machine one notch thinner,
and roll the clay through again.

7   After forming, bake
    according to the manufac-
turer's instructions and sand with
400- through 1,000-grit wet/dry
sandpaper. Buff to a high shine.

lidded boxes

These exquisite containers look like they were lathe-turned from burled maple, a beautiful wood prized for decorative items and musical instruments. But you can create these boxes without woodworking skills—or wood!

Materials

Form for the box, like a paper towel tube, mat board scored and assembled into a square, or a thin metal sheet formed into desired shape

Paper

Masking tape

Drywall sanding screen (optional)

Wet/dry sandpaper—400 through 1,000 grit

Tools

Pasta machine

Cutting blade

Buffing wheel

BURLED RED MAPLE RECIPE
ON PAGE 76

Instructions

1. Wrap a piece of paper tightly around the form, securing it with a piece of masking tape. This will permit easy removal of the clay from the form.

2. Chop and prepare the clay as per the recipe. Roll it into a sheet long enough to wrap once around your form and as wide as your box will be tall. Wrap it around the form, gently pressing to conform to the curves or angles. Cut a butt edge and smooth the seam with short strokes of your fingertip.

3. Bake for 20 minutes at the manufacturer's recommended temperature. Allow to cool and remove from the form. If the top or bottom edge of the box is not even, smooth it by stroking it on a drywall sanding screen.

4. Roll another sheet of faux burled red maple to the thickest setting on your pasta machine. Place the baked box upside down onto the sheet of clay. Use the sides of the box as a guide and cut a piece for the lid that is slightly larger than the box. Set the lid aside, top side down.

5. Place the clay box onto the sheet of clay in the same orientation as in step 4, and press lightly to leave an impression of the rim. Remove. Use the indentation from the rim as a guide to cut a flange for the lid. Cut on the inside edge of the mark made by the rim; center the flange onto the lid and press lightly to adhere.

6. In yet another area on the sheet of clay, place the box right side up. Press gently to adhere firmly to the clay, and trim around the base to create the bottom of the box. Smooth the seam.

7. Bake the box and the lid for 30 minutes at the manufacturer's recommended temperature. When it's cool, wet-sand and buff on a wheel.

PROJECT BY **Irene Semanchuk Dean**

IV

Rocks & Stones

CINNABAR

This handsome surface appears to have been meticulously carved from cinnabar; instead it's molded from a mixture of deep red clay.

RECIPE CONTRIBUTED BY **Irene Semanchuk Dean**

Materials

Premo!—Fuchsia, Zinc Yellow, and Black

Mold release

Wet/dry sandpaper—400 and 600 grit

Soft cloth

Tools

Molds that simulate the deep carving of real cinnabar

Sculpting tools of your choice

Instructions

1 Mix 6 parts fuchsia + 1 part zinc yellow + a tiny pinch of black to create the vivid red of genuine cinnabar.

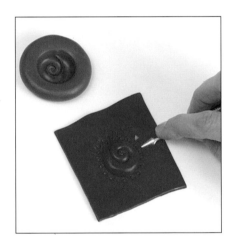

2 Apply mold release to the mold, then press the clay into the mold. Remove. As shown, add indentations with sculpting tools to enhance the "carved" effect, if desired.

3 Bake at the manufacturer's recommended temperature for at least 20 minutes.

4 When cool, wet-sand with 400- and 600-grit sandpaper. Buff by hand with a soft cloth.

TIP: Other brands of clay may be suitable for this formula, as long as the finish is not too matte.

bookends

These luxurious pieces deserve some special books—first editions, maybe, with hand illustrations and gilt lettering—to complement their special beauty. Who knows how long it might take an artisan to carve these bookends from true cinnabar? You can make them in an afternoon.

PROJECT BY **Irene Semanchuk Dean**

Materials

Heat-resistant PVA white glue

4 rectangular wooden plaques, 2 large and 2 small (from a craft store)

Wax paper (optional)

2 metal bookends

Acrylic paint—red

Felt—black

Tools

Paintbrushes

Pasta machine

Craft knife

Texture sheets

Sculpting tools

CINNABAR RECIPE ON PAGE 81

Instructions

1. Coat the front, top, and sides of the wooden plaques with glue and let dry completely.

2. Roll a sheet of the cinnabar clay to a medium thickness on the pasta machine; it should be larger than the smaller wooden plaque. Place the clay onto the small plaque, pressing to adhere it to the wood, and smooth from the center outward to eliminate air bubbles. Use a sheet of wax paper to prevent fingerprints, if desired. Wrap the clay over the top and sides of the plaque, pressing gently into place. Trim the excess clay from the back edges and from the bottom.

3. Use texture sheets to apply texture to the clay on the small plaque, working from the outer edges in toward the center. Use sculpting tools to indent additional texture if desired, as in step 2 of the recipe. Repeat for the other small plaque.

4. Bake the small plaques at 275°F (136°C) for 15 minutes. Tent the clay with aluminum foil to prevent it from darkening.

5. Repeat steps 2 and 3 to cover and texture both of the larger plaques, remembering that the center portion of each will be covered by a smaller plaque.

6. When the small plaques have cooled, place them on the large plaques, centered left to right and flush with the bottom. Trace around the perimeter with a craft knife, then remove the clay from beneath them. Apply a small amount of glue to the uncovered back of the small plaques, and set them back into place on the larger ones. Allow the glue to dry for about a half hour.

7. While the glue is drying, create many small decorative elements, using a variety of molds. Adding many pieces will create the effect of a large block of carved cinnabar. Apply these directly to the covered surfaces of the plaques, pressing firmly into place and using a rubber-tipped sculpting tool to smooth the edges of the applied pieces onto the clay beneath it.

8. When you're satisfied with your design, bake at the manufacturer's recommended temperature for 30 minutes. Tent the baking tray with aluminum foil to prevent darkening.

9. Per the recipe, sand and buff to achieve the soft sheen of cinnabar. Paint the wood on the backs of the bookends with matching red paint, allow to dry, and then glue the metal bookends into place on the back of each plaque. If necessary, glue felt pieces onto the bottoms of the bookends to protect furniture.

Jasper

Genuine jasper has a wide variety of natural states; replicate any of these distinctive variations using different combinations of colored and translucent clays.

RECIPE CONTRIBUTED BY **Luann Udell**

Materials

Polymer clay—translucent plus 4 to 6 light, medium, and dark colors, like yellow, light brown, orange, sienna, and dark brown

Wet/dry sanding sponges—fine, superfine and ultrafine grits (or the equivalent wet/dry sandpaper)

Tools

Cutting blade

Rolling pin, acrylic rod, or pasta machine

Buffing wheel or cloth

Instructions

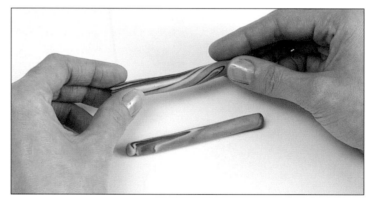

1 To begin, create two snakes of translucent clay. To one of these snakes, add separate skinny snakes of each of the light-to-medium colors. (For example, make a snake of translucent + yellow + light brown + orange.) Create another snake the same way, using the medium-to-dark colors, as shown. (For example, translucent + light brown + sienna + dark brown.)

2 Roll these snakes together, fold, and roll again. Mix until the colors are striated through the length of the snake, but don't over-mix. Mixing incompletely will create interesting bands of color throughout the translucent clay, while too much mixing will create one solid color—not what you want for this surface.

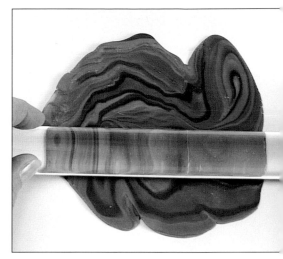

3 Make another snake from each solid color. Bundle all the snakes—translucent mixes and solid colors—into one log as shown.

4 Begin to fold, stretch and twist this log randomly. Loop the log back on itself several times to create interesting color patterns. Try folding both ends back into the middle.

5 When the color distribution is to your liking, lay the snake on a flat surface. As you lay it down, twist and turn the snake so that different colors bend in on themselves.

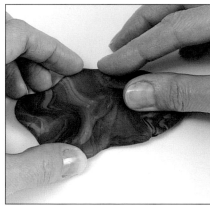

6 You can manipulate the patterns again by pushing the clay with your fingers, gently stretching, rippling, or squishing the sheet to create more patterns. Making the lines squiggle will create jasper-like or agate-like patterns.

7 When you're satisfied with the pattern, roll it out even with your rolling tool, or run it through a pasta machine. (Note that flattening the clay, especially in a pasta machine, will soften the color pattern. If you want sharp color definition, flatten the clay by hand to get the pattern you want, then lightly smooth with a rolling tool.)

8 Form the clay for your project, and bake according to the manufacturer's instructions. Sand through the grits to eliminate small irregularities and fingerprints. Buff until shiny.

cocktail cutlery

Add a sophisticated touch to your party with these elegant utensils. It's easy to transform everyday cutlery into a conversation piece by covering it with this precious stone imitation.

Materials

Assorted cutlery with plastic handles

Tools

Acrylic roller or pasta machine

Cutting blade

Needle or pin

JASPER RECIPE ON PAGE 84

Instructions

1. Prepare a sheet of faux jasper by rolling it into a sheet, or run it through a pasta machine at a medium setting.

2. Cut out a rectangle that is just longer than the handle of your utensil, and a bit wider than the circumference of the handle.

PROJECT BY **Luann Udell**

3. Gently smooth the rectangle of clay onto the handle, stroking the surface to eliminate air bubbles.

4. Trim the edges so they abut each other. Trim the clay so there's just enough to shape around the handle end. Make a smooth edge where the handle meets the utensil.

5. Check for air bubbles. Prick any you see with a needle or pin, and gently press out the air.

6. Use your finger to gently stroke the seam to make it smooth. Stroke all along the handle to make sure the clay tightly grips the utensil's surface. (This also helps eliminate fingerprints.) Repeat steps 2 through 6 for each utensil you plan to make.

7. When the surface is shaped and smoothed to your liking, bake the cutlery according to the clay manufacturer's instructions. Let cool. Sand and finish according to the recipe instructions.

TIP: Metal can be difficult to cover, so look for cutlery with riveted plastic handles like these.

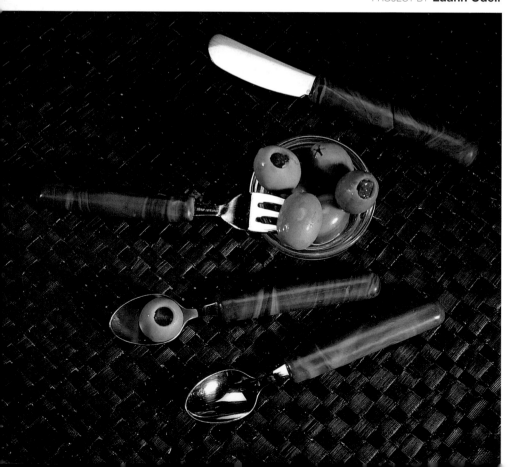

SLATE

The cool, understated look of slate, with its layers and subtle grain, is achieved through a combination of tearing, texturing, and painting the clay.

RECIPE CONTRIBUTED BY **Diane Villano**

Materials

Strong polymer clay—black

Plain white copy paper

Wax paper

Acrylic paint—black and white

Paper towels

Tools

Pasta machine or roller

Acrylic roller or brayer

Small container

Paintbrush (optional)

Instructions

1 Roll out three or four sheets of black clay to a medium thickness; all should be approximately the same width.

2 The clay must be leached (see page 14) for several hours or overnight to permit the torn edge in the next step.

3 Tear a thin strip from the top and bottom edges of one of the clay sheets, as shown. If the resulting edge looks stretched, not torn, the clay may need to be leached for a longer time. Repeat for the desired number of sheets of clay, making each successive sheet just a bit shorter than the previous sheet.

4 Crumple a sheet of wax paper, and then smooth it out. Place the wax paper on one of the clay sheets and roll over it with your brayer or roller to transfer the texture. Repeat for the other sheets of clay.

5 Stack the sheets of clay together as desired and bake according to the manufacturer's instructions. Let them cool.

6 Mix together the black and white acrylic paint to produce a gray color that appeals to you. Working on a small area at a time, apply the paint to the baked sheets, as shown. Let the paint sink into the surface texture, but immediately wipe off the excess with paper towels. Repeat for the entire piece, and don't forget to paint the edges, too. Let the paint dry.

wall clock

The minimalist design of this clock allows the beauty of its surface to be the dominant feature. The number marks themselves are made from black clay gilded with mica powder.

Materials

Clock movement and hands (with hanger)

Polymer clay—black

Cyanoacrylate glue

Sandpaper—rough grit

Mica powder—gold

Balsa wood for backing, the thickness determined by the shaft of the clock movement

Acrylic paint—black

Tools

Ruler

Craft knife

Pasta machine

Drill and bits, in the appropriate size

Paintbrush

SLATE RECIPE ON PAGE 87

Instructions

1. Roll out three or four sheets of black clay per the recipe instructions; they should be as wide as your pasta machine—approximately 5 to 6 inches (12.7 cm to 15.2 cm)—and 8 to 10 inches (20.3 to 25.4 cm) long.

2. Prepare the faux surface according to the recipe. Before baking and painting, cut a hole in the center of the clay assembly to accommodate the shaft of the clock mechanism.

3. For the number marks, roll out a small piece of black clay at a thin setting, about $\frac{1}{2}$ x 2 inches (1.3 x 5 cm). Texture by pressing with rough sandpaper and apply the gold mica powder. Bake the clay according to the manufacturer's instructions and brush off any excess mica powder. Cut the clay into number marks that appeal to you; in this project, the marks for 12, 3, 6, and 9 o'clock are a bit wider than the others. Glue the number marks to the clock face with cyanoacrylate glue.

4. Use the craft knife to cut the balsa wood to the appropriate size for the clock. Drill a hole in the center for the clock mechanism shaft. If the shaft is not long enough for the clay and the wood together, cut a hole in the wood to inset the entire mechanism. Paint the backing with black acrylic paint. When dry, glue it into place with cyanoacrylate glue.

5. Assemble the clock movement and hands according to the manufacturer's instructions.

PROJECT BY **Diane Villano**

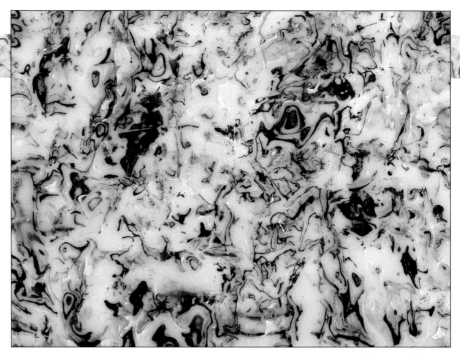

MARBLE

This beautiful rendition of marble achieves its realistic look by layering thin slices of clay onto a background sheet.

RECIPE CONTRIBUTED BY **Heather Roselli**

Materials

Fimo Soft—Translucent

Deli wrap or wax paper

Lumiere Paints—Black, Silver, and White

Cotton swab

Cornstarch

Polymer clay—white

Wet/dry sandpaper—400 through 1,000 grit

Tools

Pasta machine

Brayer

Objects for distressing, like a golf tee, shape cutters, etc.

Cutting blade

Buffing wheel

Instructions

1 Roll out thin sheets of conditioned translucent clay, using deli or wax paper to make really thin sheets that don't rip in the pasta machine. Cut eight sheets.

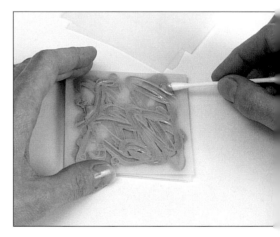

2 Begin stacking the sheets and apply paint randomly with a cotton swab, as shown. End the stack with an unpainted sheet of clay.

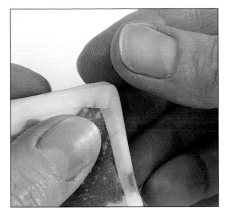

3 Cut the stack in half and place one half on top of the other. Wrap the sides of the stack with thin strips of clay, as shown, so the paint can't escape. Roll the stack with the brayer to adhere the sheets.

4 Coat the objects for distressing with cornstarch, then distress the stack by pressing the objects into it from the top and bottom. Compress the stack from the sides to re-block

between every few objects, and again after the last object. Then, allow the stack to rest and cool.

5 Press the stack firmly to your work surface to adhere it, and slice paper-thin pieces from the top of the stack, as for mokume gane.

6 Apply slices of the marble pattern to the white clay as shown. After each layer of slices, lay a sheet of wax paper over the slices and burnish them to the background and to one another by rolling lightly with a brayer. Use several layers of slices to cover the white sheet completely. Run the finished sheet through the pasta machine to the desired thickness, turning the sheet 90° after each pass to prevent distortion in one direction.

7 Bake for 30 minutes at 275°F (136°C). Straight from the oven, transfer the baked pieces to ice water to enhance the translucency of the clay; omit this step if you're covering a glass object.

8 Wet-sand all surfaces until completely smooth, and buff to a high shine.

lidded vessel

This container has a clean contemporary look while boasting a classic design. The weight of a glass votive adds to the illusion of a true marble jar.

Materials

Large glass votive

Wax paper

Polymer clay—white

Plastic wrap

Translucent liquid polymer clay

Sheet of card stock

Tools

Cutting blade

Burnishing tool, like a bone folder or a spoon

Smooth jar lid or piece of acrylic sheet

Smooth tile or glass surface

Circle cutter

MARBLE RECIPE ON PAGE 90

Instructions

1. To make the jar, create a medium thickness faux marble sheet; cut a piece that is ½ inch (1.3 cm) taller and 3 inches (7.6 cm) wider than the glass votive. Wrap the sheet around the votive, removing any air bubbles and butting the seams; trim and set

PROJECT BY **Heather Roselli**

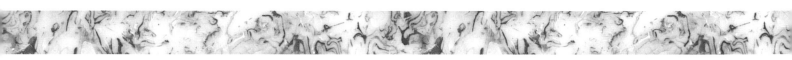

the remaining sheet aside. Cover the seams with one or two more slices from the faux marble slab and burnish flat. Cut a circle from the remaining sheet to cover the bottom of the votive, using the votive as a guide. Apply to the bottom and smooth the seams.

2. Place a small piece of wax paper on the jar and burnish the clay through the wax paper using the bone folder or the back of a spoon. Move the wax paper from section to section, burnishing the entire surface to smoothness. Put your fingers or fist inside the votive while you're working to avoid touching the clay on the outside.

3. Trim the clay flush along the top of the votive.

4. Bake the vessel for 30 minutes at 275°F (136°C). Let cool. Sand and buff as instructed in the recipe.

5. To build the lid, first make a knob by forming a small ball of white clay and covering it with faux marble slices. Roll until

completely smooth. Shape as desired, then press one end of the knob flat. Place it on the tile and bake for 20 minutes at 275°F (136°C). Let cool.

6. Create a medium-thick sheet of faux marble and apply it to a thick sheet of white clay.

7. Turn the votive upside down and lightly press the rim into the clay sheet. Remove the votive and cut along the inside of the impression. Smooth the edges and set this piece aside; it will be the flange of the lid.

8. Choose a circle cutter at least ½ inch (1.3 cm) larger in diameter than the jar opening. Place plastic wrap over the clay sheet and cut out the lid (plastic wrap between the cutter and the clay will create a beveled edge). Remove the wrap and smooth the edges.

9. Flip over the lid and center the flange onto the bottom of the lid. Press firmly into place, without distorting the shapes or edges.

10. Flip over the lid again and apply liquid clay to the flat bottom of the baked knob. Center the knob on the lid and press firmly. Bake flat on cardstock for 30 minutes at 275°F (136°C). When cool, sand and buff as directed in the recipe.

AGATE

To imitate natural agate's diverse color palette, experiment with varied color combinations.

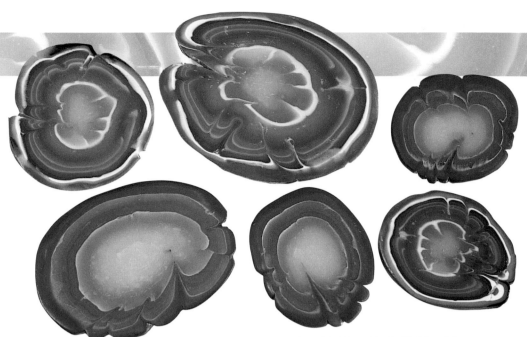

RECIPE CONTRIBUTED BY **Pat Laukkonen**

Materials

Premo!—Translucent, Raw Sienna, and White

Oil paint—white

Wet/dry sandpaper—400, 600, and 1,000 grit

Tools

Pasta machine

Cotton swab or paintbrush

Craft knife or cutting blade

Credit card or similar tool

Buffing wheel

Instructions

1 Divide the translucent clay into three approximately equal portions. Mix a very small pinch of raw sienna into one; you only want the faintest hint of color for this layer. Add a little more raw sienna to another third of translucent, making it slightly darker than your first color. Set these pieces aside and make a snake from the remaining translucent, as shown.

Make it as long as you want the cane to be, and about ¼ inch (6 mm) in diameter. Set it aside.

2 Run the lighter raw sienna mixture through the pasta machine on the widest setting. In preparation for making a bull's-eye cane, cut a piece to wrap around the translucent snake once. Smear the top with a very thin layer of white oil paint and set aside to dry. Make another slightly longer rectangle from the darker raw sienna mixture and add the paint as before.

3 When the paint on both pieces is dry, stack one atop the other and pass them through the pasta machine on the thickest setting. Cut the layers in half, stack them up, and run through the pasta machine again on the widest setting. Create a bull's-eye cane from the layers and the translucent snake you made in step 1.

4 Use a credit card or similar flat object to press into the cane from the side, as shown, inserting nearly to the center. Do this several times in close proximity and then move to a different part of the cane to repeat the process. Now, roll the cane on your work surface a few times to smooth the outside layer.

5 Continue to add layers to the bull's-eye cane, first adding a wide layer of translucent and then a sandwich of the two raw sienna shades and the translucent; run through the pasta machine at the widest setting. Make the layers thicker as you work outward. Use the

credit card again to create indentations in the outside of the cane as in step 4, and roll on your work surface to smooth the outside. Add another layer of colors if you like; since the layers should be getting thicker, don't double-stack before passing through the pasta machine. Distress the stack as before.

6 Allow the cane to rest before slicing, as translucent can easily become overworked. Slice the faux agate cane and bake the slices according to the manufacturer's instructions. When cool, wet-sand and buff for a light shine.

ornaments

Let the light shine through these translucent slices of faux agate. Use jewelry findings to create a set of unique ornaments.

Materials

Wet/dry sandpaper—400, 600, and 1,000 grit

Pendant bails (from a beading store or findings supplier)

Cyanoacrylate glue (optional)

Beading silk or similar material, like metallic thread or thin ribbon

Tools

Cutting blade

Pasta machine

Needle tool

Buffing wheel

AGATE RECIPE ON PAGE 94

Instructions

1. Cut slices from several different logs of faux agate to provide variety. Don't slice the pieces too thinly, though—they should be just thick enough to flatten nicely on the first setting of the pasta machine without distorting.

2. If necessary, use the needle tool to make a small hole in one end of each agate slice to accommodate a bail, which will be added in step 4.

3. Bake following the manufacturer's instructions. When cool, wet-sand and buff to a high shine.

4. Insert the bails in each slice of agate, or glue them on if appropriate. Tie on the beading silk. Vary the length of the silk for visual interest.

Variations: You can experiment with the appearance of your faux agate slices by cutting them a little thicker and then running them through the pasta machine.

There are several other project ideas for these faux agate slices: Use a piece of found wood to create a mobile, or mount them on a votive holder—the candlelight shining through will make the agates gleam.

PROJECT BY **Pat Laukkonen**

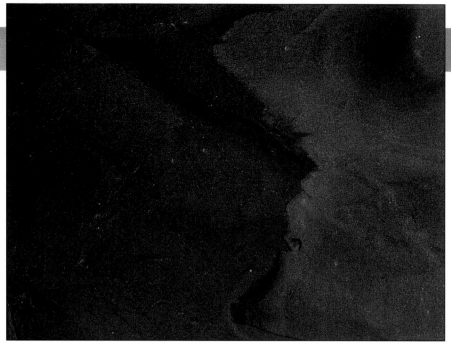

RIVER ROCK

Simulate the subtle texture of river rock smoothed by years of rushing water; it's surprisingly simple.

Materials

Premo!—Black and Translucent

Pearl Ex—Silver and Gold

Sculpey Diluent

Tools

Pasta machine

Cutting blade

RECIPE CONTRIBUTED BY **Pat Pettyjohn**

Instructions

1 Roll the black clay into a 3-inch-wide (7.6 cm) strip at a medium setting on the pasta machine and set aside.

2 Divide the translucent clay in half, and roll each half into a sheet. Spread three to four drops of diluent on each sheet, then tint one with gold mica powder and the other with silver, as shown. The diluent will keep the mica powders from becoming airborne.

3 Fold and run each sheet through the pasta machine until fully blended, then roll each sheet into a 3-inch-wide (7.6 cm) strip at a medium setting.

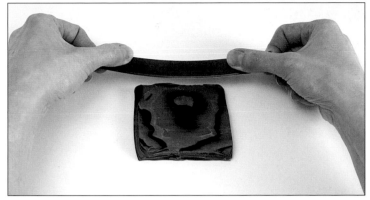

4 Sandwich the black strip between the silver and the gold sheets, and run the stack through the pasta machine at its thickest setting. Run through again at a medium setting. Divide the strip into sections that are approximately 3 inches (7.6 cm) square, and stack.

5 Bending your blade slightly, as shown, remove a thick, uneven slice (about $\frac{1}{8}$ inch [3 mm]) from the top. Run this uneven slice through the pasta machine at the thickest setting; skip a setting or two, then run through again at a medium setting. Skip down to a very thin setting. Be sure to skip the settings as indicated, because this action will make the clay pull through the machine faster on one side than the other, resulting in a sheet that is smooth on one side and slightly textured on the other, with soft waves of color running through. It can be folded and run through again until desired results are achieved.

6 Bake according to the manufacturer's instructions. No sanding or buffing is needed.

pendant with abstract bail

This exquisite pendant, shown at the left on the opposite page, features faux river rock pebbles in a matching frame. Sterling silver findings add a touch of elegant simplicity.

Materials

Polymer clay—black

Sterling silver wire, 14- or 16-gauge

Cyanoacrylate glue

1 yard (.9 m) of rayon or neoprene cord—black

Tools

Pasta machine

Cutting blade

Craft knife

Jig

Wire cutters

Pliers (optional)

Rawhide hammer

Pin vise, with bits to match sizes of your wire

RIVER ROCK RECIPE ON
PAGE 98

Instructions

1. Using the thickest setting of the pasta machine, roll out two 2 x 3-inch (5 x 6.4 cm) sheets of black clay and stack them together. Roll one more sheet at a medium setting. Set it aside.

2. Look at your sheet of the faux surface, and find an area with desirable color variation. Cut out a rectangle approximately 1¾ x 2½ inches (4.4 x 6.4 cm).

3. Gently roll this rectangle of faux river rock onto the stack of black clay you made in step 1. Cut out a smaller rectangle from within, leaving a border of at least ½ inch (1.3 cm) to create a frame. Place the frame onto the remaining sheet of black clay and trim the outside of the rectangle as desired.

4. Make three small irregularly shaped pebbles from leftover black clay. Cover each pebble with the faux surface. Place the pebbles inside the frame and press gently to adhere them to the black clay. Bake at 275°F (136°C) for 30 minutes.

5. To finish the pendant, use the jig to create an abstract wire bail. (Just bend it with pliers, if you prefer). When you're happy with the design, remove it from the jig and hammer it flat with a rawhide hammer. Make a loop at the top for the cording. Drill a small hole in the top of the pendant, add glue to the end of the wire, and insert into the hole. Add black rayon or neoprene cord and knot to complete.

Alternatives: You can create many variations with this basic idea. If you're experienced with soldering, you can embellish the pendant as shown at the right on page 101, and then attach a cord with a loop and bead closure. (Make the beads from the faux surface, too.) This pendant also features a background of the faux river rock, rather than black clay. Lastly, use the faux surface to create your own "stone," as shown in the center of the photo.

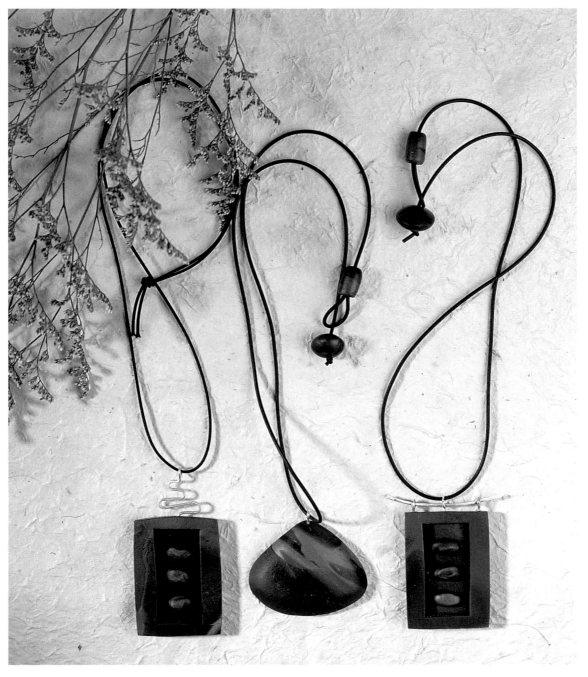

PROJECT BY **Pat Pettyjohn**

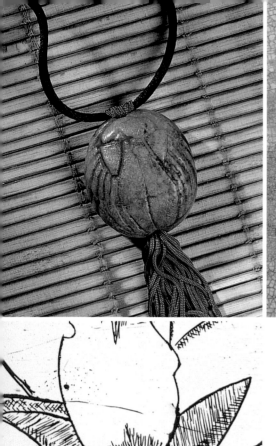
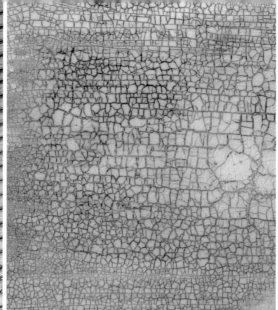

V

Surface Decoration

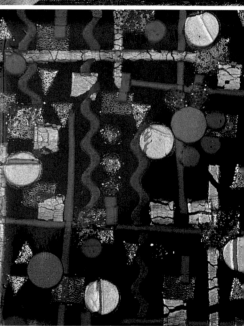

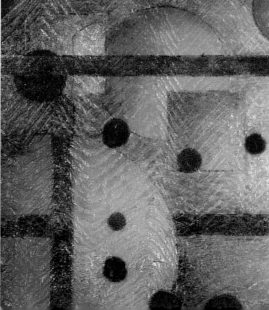
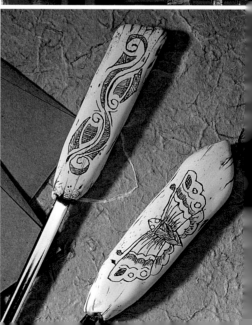

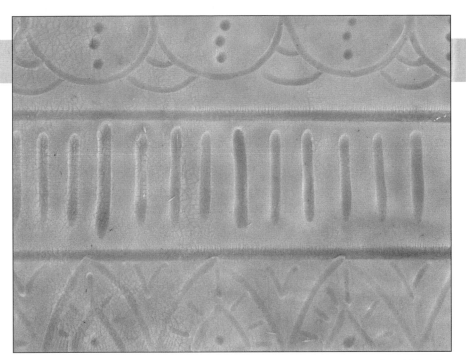

CELADON

One of the secrets for achieving the appearance of a celadon glaze is to apply the colored liquid clay in several thin layers.

RECIPE CONTRIBUTED BY **Gerri Newfry**

Materials

Polymer clay—white

Powdered Pearls—Jade

Translucent liquid polymer clay

Sculpey Diluent (optional)

One-step crackle medium

Tools

Pasta machine or acrylic roller

Blunt tool for carving, like a paintbrush handle

Paintbrushes

Container

Instructions

1 Roll a sheet of white polymer clay to ⅛ inch (3 mm) thick. Mold your piece or cover an object as desired, and carve the clay with geometric or floral designs as shown. Don't worry about creating an irregular surface, because that just adds to the appeal of the final product.

2 Bake according to the manufacturer's instructions.

3 Mix the mica powder with the liquid clay until it reaches the desired very pale to pale green color of true celadon, about 1 part mica powder + 16 parts liquid clay. Add the diluent if necessary; the mixture should have the consistency of buttermilk. Paint the mixture onto the white baked surface, allowing the tinted liquid clay to accumulate in the impressed areas; use a fairly thin coat that pools a bit, yet doesn't drip.

4 To cure the liquid clay, bake according to the manufacturer's instructions. Apply the tinted liquid clay two to four more times until the desired shade is reached, baking after each application of the mixture. To finish your piece, varnish with the crackle medium according to the manufacturer's instructions, as shown.

miniature vase

This project's decoration is very similar to the traditional *shinogi* technique, in which designs are carved deeply into the ceramic ware before the glaze is applied. The carvings allow the glaze to pool, just as in this faux process.

Materials

Glass vase or bottle

CELADON RECIPE ON PAGE 103

Instructions

1. Cover the glass vessel with the layer of clay, making sure to avoid any bubbles between the glass and clay. Smooth the seams with your fingers.

2. Embellish the surface as described in the recipe, adding decoration as desired.

3. When your vase is cool, finish as directed in step 4 of the surface recipe.

PROJECT BY **Gerri Newfry**

DICHROIC GLASS

The brilliant color play of dichroic glass is seen here in the shimmer of this imitative clay surface, which is created with leafing foil and mica powders.

RECIPE CONTRIBUTED BY **Elizabeth Campbell**

Materials

Premo!—CFC06 (Translucent 1310 with bleach) and Black

Mica powders in your preferred colors

Wax paper, tracing paper, or deli wrap

Composition metal leaf

Heat-resistant micro glitters in your preferred colors

Nitrile gloves

Wet/dry sandpaper—320 through 800 grit

Polymer-friendly varnish—glossy

Tools

Pasta machine

Shape cutters (from a craft store) or canapé cutters

Cutting blade

Ceramic tile

Small acrylic rod or brayer

Buffing wheel

Instructions

1 Using the CFC06 and a variety of mica powders, create small amounts of differently colored mixtures. Mix the powder thoroughly into each batch of clay and roll through the pasta machine several times to align the mica particles. Roll these sheets to the thinnest setting possible, as shown, using tracing paper or deli wrap if the clay is sticky. Set aside.

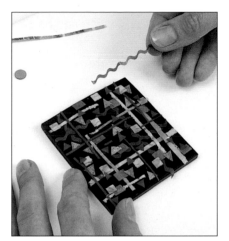

2 Roll some additional CFC06, with no powder inclusions, through the pasta machine at the thinnest setting possible. Apply decorative foils or glitters to one side of these sheets.

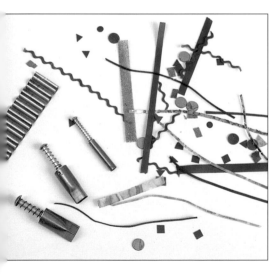

3 Cut various shapes from both the colored clays created in step 1 and the foil or glitter sheets you made in step 2. Set these decorative elements aside.

4 Create a base sheet from the black clay that is much larger than your final piece; make this sheet by rolling two sheets from the thickest setting on your pasta machine. Stack the two sheets together on the ceramic tile, and roll an acrylic rod back and forth over them to adhere them to each other. Place the decorative pieces you made in step 3 in the middle of this base sheet and arrange them to your liking; it's okay to overlap some of the pieces. The mica-colored clay can be placed face-up or face-down, but the pieces with foil or glitter should be applied with the foil or glitter face-down on the clay.

5 When you're happy with the arrangement, cover the clay with a piece of wax paper, tracing paper, or deli wrap. With your acrylic rod, sweep over the clay as shown to adhere the decorative elements to the base sheet, as well as the paper to the design. This keeps the design elements from distorting. (Be sure to sweep, rather than roll, in this step.) Peel off the paper and check the design. If you see any seams, roll across them gently to bring the edges together.

6 Cut out the shape needed for your project and remove the excess clay. Slide this piece off the tile with a blade; handle it wearing gloves for extra protection against fingerprints. Roll down the edges of the piece with a small rod or brayer to create a beveled edge all around. Smooth the outside edges of the design. Curve the piece if desired and repair any seams. Place the piece face-down on paper, batting, or other non-reflective surface, and bake for 30 minutes at 275°F (136°C). (The baking time may vary depending upon your project.)

7 After cooling, sand (and sand and sand!) with 320- or 400-grit wet/dry sandpaper. You want to remove a lot of material, nearly all of the translucent clay that's on top of the glitter or foil. For instance, if your colored pieces were rolled at the #7 setting on your pasta machine, you'll be removing around one half its thickness in the sanding process. Continue sanding using progressively finer sandpaper, up to 800 grit or more. Buff and apply glossy varnish.

compact

Create any number of accessories featuring this gorgeous surface that appears to change colors as the light dances off the elements. If you can bear to part with this piece, it would make a memorable gift for a special person.

Materials

Premo!—Black

Compact

Nitrile gloves

Silicone or cyanoacrylate glue

Rubbing alcohol

Paper towels

Tools

Pasta machine

Cutting blade

Acrylic rod or brayer

Scalpel or needle tool

DICHROIC GLASS RECIPE ON PAGE 106

Instructions

1. One side of the mirror compact used in this project has a shallow "well." To fill it, roll out black or scrap clay on about the third-thickest setting on your pasta machine. Cut a circle from the clay to fit into the well. Press it into the well and smooth it with an acrylic brayer.

2. Roll out a sheet of black clay on the thickest setting of your pasta machine; the sheet should be big enough to cover the top and bottom of your compact. Roll it onto a ceramic tile or piece of glass as directed in the surface recipe, and follow the instructions to embellish the clay with decorative elements.

3. Using the compact as a template, cut two circles from the decorated black clay. Wear gloves as you apply a circle to one side of the compact, smoothing from the center to the outside edges. Ease the clay over the edge and smooth it down to the lip of the compact. You'll need to trim off the excess flush with the inside of that lip, and you may need to trim out the area around the latch or the hinge. Use a small brayer to smooth the upper surface and the sides.

4. Bake for 15 minutes at 275°F (136°C).

5. Apply the remaining circle to the other side of the compact as in step 3, and bake again for 30 minutes at 275°F (136°C). While the compact is still warm, remove the clay pieces by sliding a scalpel or needle tool under the edges all around and then peeling the clay from the compact. Be careful not to scratch the metal plating. If the mirror loosened during baking, secure it with a dab of silicone or cyanoacrylate gel glue. Clean the outside of the compact with rubbing alcohol and set aside.

6. Sand and buff the pieces as directed in the surface instructions. Buff the outsides of the pieces on slow speed with rather firm pressure, and then on high speed using very little pressure.

7. Apply two or more coats of varnish as directed in the recipe, let dry for at least 24 hours. Use glue to place the decorated covers on the compact.

PROJECT BY **Elizabeth Campbell**

FAIENCE

This technique creates the look of ancient Egyptian faience, with its once-vivid opaque glazes that have been weathered through the centuries.

RECIPE CONTRIBUTED BY **Elizabeth Campbell**

Materials

Premo!—CFC06 (Translucent 5310 with bleach)

Piñata Inks—Sunbright Yellow, Chile Pepper Red, Burro Brown, and Rainforest Green

Mica powder—silver

Translucent liquid polymer clay

Additional mica powders and inks in your preferred colors

Toothpick

Wet/dry sandpaper—320 through 800 grit (optional)

Polymer-friendly varnish—satin (optional)

Tools

Scalpel

Bulb syringe

Containers

Paintbrushes

Buffing wheel (optional)

Instructions

1 To tint the small amount of clay needed for this surface, use this method: Roll a small piece of CFC06 into a sheet, apply the inks to one surface as shown, and let dry. The green and brown inks will tone down the brightness of the reds and produce a slightly muted orange. Let the inks dry and mix into the clay.

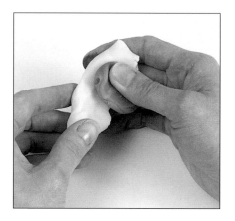

2 Use bits of the tinted clay to color an appropriate amount of the CFC06 for your project; the final color should resemble pale peach or apricot.

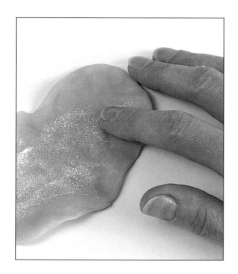

3 Mix some silver mica powder into the mixture you made in step 2.

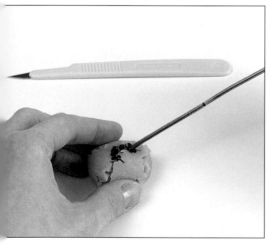

4 Now, form the clay into the design of your choice. Add some age cracks by tearing into the piece with a pointed

scalpel and dripping a reddish-brown ink mix into the crevices you've created, as shown. Let the ink dry and close up the cracks, then shape and add detail to the piece as desired.

5 Bake the pieces at 275°F (136°C) for 20 to 30 minutes, and carve further, if desired.

6 Tint the translucent liquid polymer clay with the inks and powders to create colors that the Egyptians used—like lapis blue, turquoise blue, burnt sienna, ochre, and umber. Allow the ink to sit on top of the liquid clay for 30 minutes to allow the alcohol to evaporate, then use a toothpick to mix each color.

Paint your piece with these mixtures as shown, keeping the paints in the crevices to mimic the effects of two thousand years of aging. Begin with the darkest colors, but keep the paint job spotty, allowing plenty of the bare surface to remain.

7 Bake for about 10 minutes at 300°F (150°C) and let cool. Repeat the painting step if desired. Finish as you choose; if you prefer a more realistic finish, no sanding is required. For a high gloss, wet-sand at length and buff to a shine. Finish with varnish, if you wish.

scarab pendant

Capture the look of ancient Egypt using modern materials.
Add faux faience beads to this stunning scarab for a necklace
a pharaoh would be proud to wear.

Materials

Nitrile gloves

1 yard (.9 m) of 2 or 3 mm satin rattail cord—black

2 to 3 feet (1.8 to 2.7 m) of rayon yarn—turquoise

Twist tie

Clasp (optional)

Tools

Metal knitting needle, 4 or 5 mm

Cutting blade

Disposable scalpel or wax sculpting tool

Scissors

FAIENCE RECIPE ON PAGE 110

Instructions

1. With gloved hands, roll a lump of prepared faux faience into a smooth oval shape, and then press it down into a domed oval cabochon. Pierce the knitting needle into the oval from top to bottom, lengthwise. Use the cutting blade to slide it off the work surface, leaving the knitting needle in place.

2. Using the dull side of the blade, press it around the bottom edge of the oval, creating a rim all around the outside edge that's about $1/16$ inch (1.6 mm) deep.

3. Detail your scarab with simple lines for the head, wings, and legs with the dull side of the scalpel or a wax sculpting tool. You can carve or stamp an Egyptian symbol on the back of the scarab to imitate the ancient seal amulets.

4. Bake the scarab for 30 minutes at 275°F (136°C). Let cool.

5. Color and finish as described in the recipe. Remove the knitting needle when you've finished this step.

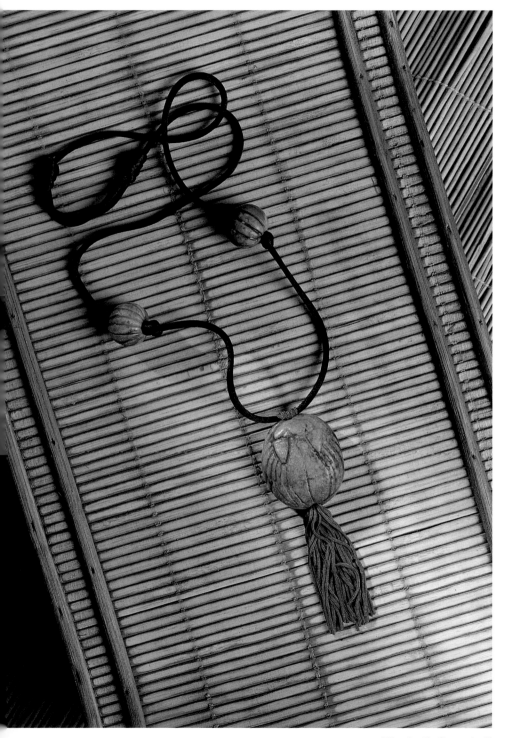

6. To create the pendant, cut an appropriate length of black rattail cord and set aside. Wrap the turquoise rayon yarn around your hand several times to get a bunch of 6 to 10 loops that are about 4 to 5 inches (10.2 to 12.7 cm) in diameter. Slip a twist tie into the bunch and twist it. Thread the tie into the scarab to see if the yarn bundle fits snugly, but can still be pulled through the hole without too much difficulty. If it doesn't feed through the pendant fairly easily, remove the bundle, take off one or two loops, bundle with the twist tie, and try again. Conversely, if the scarab doesn't fit snugly on the yarn without sliding, remove the yarn bundle, add a strand or two, and try again. When the yarn bundle fits well, pull it through far enough to thread the rattail cord onto the loops of yarn at the top of the pendant.

7. Remove the twist tie and pull on the bottom of the yarn bundle so it tightens down on the cord. Trim off the bottom of the yarn to create a tassel of the desired length, and attach a clasp or knot the cord as desired.

PROJECT BY **Elizabeth Campbell**

Cloisonné

The vivid hues of cloisonné are achieved using translucent liquid polymer clay tinted into a rainbow of colors.

RECIPE CONTRIBUTED BY **Heather Roselli**

Materials

Cloisonné pattern (see figure 1)

Tracing paper

Polymer clay—white

Wet/dry sandpaper—400 grit

Leafing pen—gold or silver

Oil paints in the colors of your choice

Toothpicks

Translucent liquid polymer clay

Polymer-friendly varnish—glossy

Tools

Pencil

Linoleum or rubber carving block

Linoleum block cutter with a #1 V-shaped blade

Pasta machine

Brayer

Craft knife

Ball stylus or clay shaper

Small glass or plastic containers

1 mL syringes with 22-gauge needles, one for each color

Instructions

1 Trace your chosen pattern onto tracing paper with the pencil. Turn face-down onto the carving block. Burnish with your fingernail or trace over the drawing with a pencil to transfer the design to the carving block. You can also draw directly onto the carving block if desired.

Figure 1

2 Carve the design with the V-shaped gouge, as shown. Carve as deeply as the top of the gouge allows, using even pressure. To carve curves and circles, rotate the block rather than the carving handle. For small circles and other areas too small to carve, gouge out the area completely; later, use a small ball stylus to shape an inner cell in the clay. Remove any rubber crumbs from the grooves of mold by pressing scrap clay into the design.

3 After conditioning, roll the white clay through the pasta machine on the widest setting. Lay the sheet over the mold you've carved and press the clay firmly into all areas of the mold with your fingers. Roll over the clay with a brayer until smooth. Carefully and slowly pull the clay from the mold, as shown, and place it flat onto a surface for baking. Cut around the perimeter of the design with a sharp craft knife. Fix any imperfections in the cell walls or floors with a ball stylus or clay shaper. Use the stylus to open up any small areas in the clay that were gouged out in the mold. Bake for 20 minutes at 275° (136°C).

4 When cool, lightly wet-sand the surface of the raised design with 400-grit sandpaper to even out and flatten the tops of the cell walls. When dry, use the leafing pen to apply a metallic finish to the tops of cell walls and to the outside edges of the piece, as shown. Allow to dry thoroughly.

5 In the small containers, add a small dab of oil paint from the end of a toothpick to 1 or 2 teaspoons (5 or 10 mL) of translucent liquid polymer clay; repeat for each color desired. Mix each color thoroughly with a toothpick.

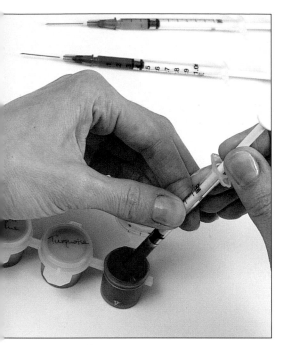

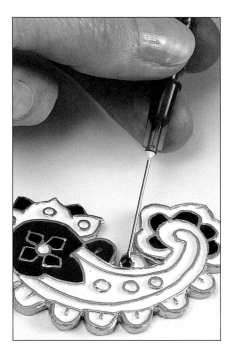

6 Draw the colored liquid clay into syringes without the needle attached, as shown. Then attach the needle and slowly dispense the colored clay into the desired cell of the baked piece. (Press lightly on the syringe and be patient, for too much pressure will cause the needle to blow off.)

7 Fill cells carefully until the liquid clay is just slightly domed up over the cell, but don't allow it to contact or overflow into the neighboring cell. After all the cells are filled with the desired colors, allow the piece to stand on a level surface for about one hour. Pop any bubbles that form with a sharp pin or needle.

8 Bake the piece on a level baking surface for 30 minutes at 300°F (150°C). This higher temperature is necessary to cure the liquid polymer clay.

9 Use the leafing pen to touch up any areas as necessary. When dry, coat the entire piece with varnish, letting it dry completely between coats.

Alternative: Instead of carving your own design, look for a rubber stamp with very deep impressions; a purchased stamp will simplify this recipe.

TIP: The translucent liquid clay will thicken as it ages. If you need to thin it, use a small amount of diluent, but be careful to add just a tiny bit at a time.

paisley brooch

This lively paisley is the perfect motif for the cloisonné technique, which features many separate cells of color. Add a pin back to create a distinctive piece of jewelry.

Materials

Pin back

Cyanoacrylate glue

Translucent liquid polymer clay

Polymer clay—white

Cotton or polyester batting or fiberfill

Metallic leafing pen that matches the color used on the faux cloisonné

Polymer-friendly varnish—glossy

CLOISONNE RECIPE ON PAGE 114

Instructions

1. Prepare your faux cloisonné piece according to the surface recipe, using the featured design on page 114 or your own sketch. Once your piece is cool, turn it over and glue on the pin back so it stays in place while you work.

2. Cover the base of the pin back with a thin layer of liquid clay, and then add a thin square of white clay over the pin back to secure it in place. Make sure that the clay square is thin enough to allow the pin to open and close.

3. Place the brooch pin side down on some batting, surrounding the pin back with extra batting so that the brooch lies level. Bake for 30 minutes at 275°F (136°C). Let cool.

4. Use the leafing pen to color the back of the brooch and to touch up other areas as necessary. When the brooch is dry, coat it with varnish.

PROJECT BY **Heather Roselli**

RAKU

The distinctive fine cracks of traditional raku pottery, developed in sixteenth-century Japan, are imitated with remarkable accuracy in just a few simple steps.

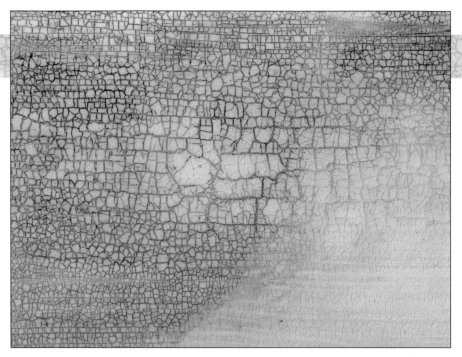

RECIPE CONTRIBUTED BY **Lynn Krucke**

Materials

Polymer clay—white and beige

Anita's Fragile Crackle

Acrylic paint—black

Paper towel or soft cloth

Polymer-friendly glaze (optional)

Tools

Clay roller or pasta machine (optional)

Cutting blade

Paintbrush

Instructions

1 Mix 4 parts white + 1 part beige. Use the clay mixture to form, mold, or cover the piece for your project. Bake according to the manufacturer's instructions.

2 After the clay has cooled, apply the crackle finish to the surface of the baked clay, following the manufacturer's instructions carefully. You must use a two-part crackle product; be advised that the crackles will be unpredictable.

3 After the crackles have appeared, apply the paint sparingly—rub a small amount of black acrylic paint onto the surface of the clay with small circular motions to highlight the cracks. You can pick and choose the areas that you wish to highlight.

4 Use a paper towel or clean cloth to wipe off the excess paint. If too much black paint remains on the surface, wet the cloth and wipe again.

5 If a glossy finish is desired, varnish with one or more coats of a polymer-friendly glaze.

Alternative: Depending upon your desired project, you could also sand the baked surface before adding the crackle medium. See the lamp project on page 120 for more details.

table lamp

A lamp like this one in genuine raku might be hard to come by, but creating your own imitation is simpler than you might think. Lovely, isn't it?

Materials

Small purchased ceramic lamp

Heat-resistant PVA white glue

Sculpey Diluent

Nitrile gloves (optional)

Wet/dry sandpaper—320, 400, and 600 grit

Tools

Tools for rewiring the lamp (see note below)

Paintbrush

Pasta machine

Craft knife

RAKU RECIPE ON PAGE 118

Note: Rewiring a lamp is not a difficult task, but it does require some basic knowledge of electrical wiring. Your lamp's specific construction will determine the procedure, as well as dictate which tools you'll need. Please refer to a home-improvement manual or a similar resource for specific instructions.

Instructions

1. Disassemble the lamp and remove the wiring; you'll be working with the ceramic base. Mark the wires and the socket as you take the lamp apart, to make re-assembly easier. Set aside the wiring.

2. Paint a thin layer of the glue over the entire surface of the lamp and allow it to dry.

3. Mix the clay as described in step 1 of the recipe and roll into sheets approximately ⅛ inch (3 mm) thick. Cover the lamp completely with sheets of clay. Work on one section at a time, and press each sheet of clay carefully onto the lamp, taking care not to trap air. Make sure the clay is well-adhered to the lamp. Trim and piece the sheets as needed to cover the curves of the lamp. Smooth all seams.

4. Unlike the surface recipe, the clay in this project needs to be smoothed and sanded, because it was subjected to the stress of covering a round object. To smooth the surface of the lamp and reduce the amount of sanding you'll have to do after baking, squeeze a small amount of diluent into your hands and rub them together; you may wish to wear gloves. Smooth your hands over the surface of the lamp, gently rubbing away fingerprints and "polishing" the clay.

5. Bake the clay-covered lamp base for one hour at the manufacturer's recommended temperature.

6. After the lamp base has cooled, wet-sand it lightly with 320-grit sandpaper. Repeat with the 400- and then 600-grit sandpaper. Dry the lamp base completely.

7. Apply the crackle medium and paint as directed in the surface recipe. Finish per the recipe.

8. Rewire the lamp, using the markings you made earlier to re-attach each wire to the proper terminal on the socket.

PROJECT BY **Lynn Krucke**

Scrimshaw on Faux Ivory

Save the whales with this environmentally friendly version of scrimshaw, created using faux ivory and traditional scrimshaw carving techniques.

RECIPE CONTRIBUTED BY **Irene Semanchuk Dean**

Materials

Polymer clay—white and translucent

Wet/dry sandpaper—400 through 1,000 grit

Acrylic paint—brown and black

Paper towel

Paper (optional)

Cotton swabs

Soft cloth

Tools

Pasta machine

Craft knife with sharp blade

Pen or pencil

Pins (optional)

Instructions

1 Thoroughly mix equal parts white and translucent polymer clay and roll into a sheet. Roll another sheet of white clay, approximately the same size of the mixed sheet. Make a stack of polymer clay with an ivory "grain" by first laying one sheet on top of the other. Run it through the pasta machine, cut in half, stack and run through the pasta machine again. Repeat this process until the individual layers are paper-thin and the stack is approximately 1 inch (2.5 cm) thick, as shown.

2 Take slices from this stack and form them into the desired shape for your project. It's okay for there to be slight imperfections or nicks in the surface—this will add a realistic "old" feel to the finished piece. Bake at 275°F (136°C) for at least 30 to 40 minutes.

3 When cool, sand lightly with 400- and 600-grit sandpaper. With your finger, add

a small amount of brown acrylic paint to the surface of the faux ivory and rub it in completely, making sure to get it into any small nicks or fissures in the clay surface. Wipe the excess paint from the clay, leaving a brown stain; this will make it easier to see the lines of the image you're about to incise.

4 Draw the image you want to etch onto the faux ivory. If you prefer, you can draw an image on a piece of paper, lay it over the baked clay, and trace its outline with pinpricks. Then, remove the paper and connect the dots with a pen or pencil.

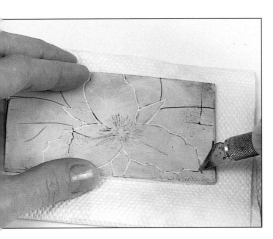

5 Hold the craft knife in a "backward" position as shown—tip down, but blade away from you, not toward you. This allows you to etch with only

the tip of the knife blade. Scribe or etch over your pencil marks by pulling the tip of the blade toward you. Work slowly and deliberately. To etch the curves, move the clay in the direction of the curve, instead of trying to curve the direction of the blade. Place the clay on something like a coaster or a folded paper towel to make these subtle turns and rotations easier.

6 When you have etched the lines of your image, scuff the surface lightly with dry 800- or 1,000-grit sandpaper to remove the burrs created by the incising. Use a cotton swab to rub black acrylic paint into the lines you've just created, as shown. Wipe off the excess with a paper towel.

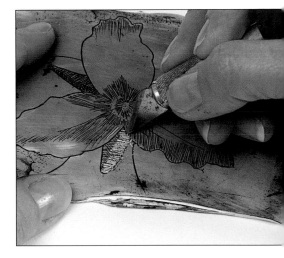

7 If you want to create shading, use the tip of the blade to etch crosshatched lines as shown—many tightly placed lines all in one direction, followed by many tightly placed lines perpendicular to those. Again, scuff off any burrs and use a cotton swab to rub black paint into the crosshatching; wipe off the excess with a paper towel.

8 Allow the paint to dry for about an hour. Then, wet-sand with 600- through 800- or 1,000-grit sandpaper. Don't over-sand! You might remove part of your design. If this happens, etch it and paint it again. Rinse the piece and dry thoroughly. Buff with a soft cloth.

letter opener

Make letter opening an artistic endeavor when you use these enchanting and well-crafted tools. A distinctive desk accessory!

PROJECT BY **Irene Semanchuk Dean**

Materials

Polymer clay—white

Metal letter opener

Heat-resistant PVA white glue

Tools

Pasta machine

Brayer or acrylic rod

SCRIMSHAW ON FAUX IVORY
RECIPE ON PAGE 122

Instructions

1. Roll a sheet of white clay at the thickest setting. Place slices from the ivory stack onto the sheet of white clay, and roll lightly with a brayer to smooth and flatten. Coat the letter opener handle with glue, allow to dry, and then cover with the faux ivory sheet you just made. Smooth the top end of the handle, but leave the end closest to the blade somewhat imperfect—so it looks a bit rough, like aged ivory or bone.

2. Bake the letter opener at the manufacturer's recommended temperature for 45 minutes. Allow it to cool.

3. Follow the recipe to create a scrimshaw design on the letter opener handle.

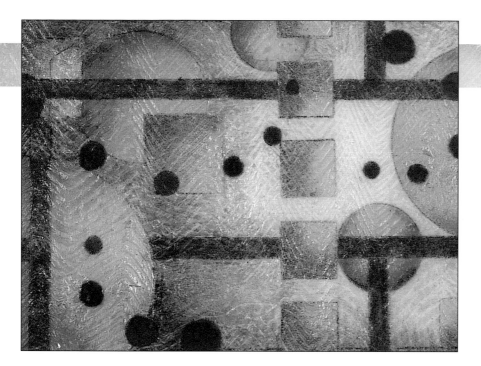

BASSE-TAILLE ENAMEL

True basse-taille enamel has textured gold or silver below layers of translucent enamel. This breathtaking surface obtains its brilliance from an underlay of silver leaf.

RECIPE CONTRIBUTED BY **Julia Sober**

Materials

Drawing on white paper (use figure 1 if desired)

Colored pencils

Translucent liquid polymer clay

White craft glue

Wax paper

Metal leaf—silver

Polymer clay—black

Tools

Scissors

Paintbrush

Piece of glass

Comb

Pasta machine

Cutting blade

Ruler

Instructions

1 Copy or draw an image for your project onto a piece of white paper, or use figure 1, and fill it in with the colored pencils. Begin by deciding which colors you will use; a balance of warm and cool color groups is visually pleasing. For each section to be colored, choose at least three pencils in a range of shades from light to dark.

2 To create the smooth shading in this surface, color each area with the lightest color first. Color in about half of the image with the lightest colored pencil for each color group, pressing hard to deposit a good layer of pigment—this will act as a resist later when removing the paper, so be sure not to leave any bare paper areas while coloring. Extend the colors past the outer edges of your design, leaving a good-sized border to aid in paper removal.

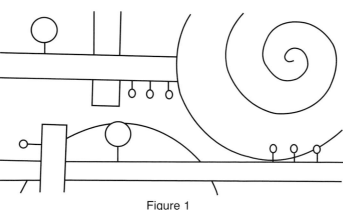

Figure 1

image colored-side up, paint a thin layer of translucent liquid polymer clay directly onto the image while you hold it by the tab, as shown. The colored image should be visible through this layer of liquid clay.

sections should be slightly blurred. If the image is clearly visible, the layer of liquid clay is probably too thin and more should be added.

3 Continue with the next darkest color—still pressing hard—blending it back over about half of the lighter color as well as advancing it into the uncolored areas of the design, as shown. However, don't forget to leave some uncolored area for the next color; continue in this manner until the whole section is shaded from light to dark. Repeat as necessary until the entire design is colored.

5 Turn the image over onto the glass, pressing down the side opposite the tab. Turn the glass over and work from the underside to gently roll the paper onto the glass with the side of your index finger, as shown, watching for air bubbles. Pull any bubbles toward the tab end as you roll the image onto the glass, and smooth any remaining bubbles gently toward the edges of the paper image. There should be an even layer of liquid clay between the paper and the glass; the colored image should be visible, but the lines between the

6 Turn the glass over and bake at 300°F (150°C) for 25 minutes; proper baking is vital. When removed from the oven and turned over, the image should be brilliantly colored, not milky, and clearly visible through the glass and liquid clay layer. After removing the clay from the oven, allow a few minutes for the image transfer to cool and let the colors set.

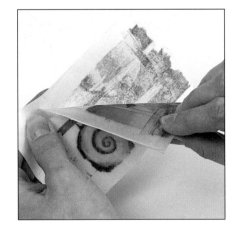

7 Peel the transfer and paper away from the glass. To remove the paper from the clay, stretch the transfer in a corner of the colored area until the paper tears. A properly cured

4 Cut out the colored image, leaving a 1-inch (2.5 cm) tab on at least one side. With the

transfer will stretch quite a bit, tearing the paper instead of the baked clay. Gently stretch the colored areas of the transfer to lift the paper away, as shown, pulling it from your image in pieces if necessary. Trim the uncolored and rough edges of the transfer with scissors, leaving extra space if the transfer will be framed in clay.

8 Apply a thin layer of glue to the colored side of the image. Let the glue set up slightly, then texture it by dragging a comb through it. Let the glue dry until it is clear.

9 Place a piece of silver leaf onto a small piece of waxed paper; the leaf should be large enough to cover the image. Apply the transfer to the leaf glue-side down, as shown, exhaling onto the glue before applying to encourage adhesion. Turn the transfer and waxed paper over, and burnish the leaf well into the grooves of the textured glue with your fingers.

10 Trim the finished surface sheet to the desired shape and size, leaving space for framing with clay if desired.

11 To use the transfer in a project, roll a sheet of black clay through the pasta machine at its thickest setting. Trim the clay sheet to the proper size for your project.

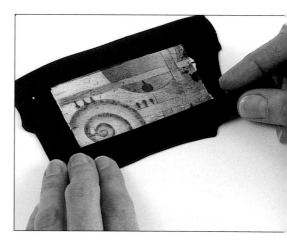

12 Apply the transfer to the base clay, leaf side down, by pressing gently. To frame the faux enameled piece, cut strips from a medium-thick sheet of black clay, using a ruler as a guide. Frame the image, applying the strips over the raw black clay and the outer edges of the image as shown. Press well and trim the edges of the frame if necessary. Bake again at 275°F (136°C) for 25 minutes.

accordion book

This dazzling book deserves to be judged by its cover. A coordinating ribbon
unties to reveal accordion-folded paper behind the luminous image,
ready to receive your brilliant thoughts or messages.

PROJECT BY **Julia Sober**

Materials

Sheet of paper, 8½ x 11 inches (21.6 x 27.9 cm)

White craft glue

Polymer clay—black

Piece of corrugated cardboard (optional)

Oven-safe ribbon

Wet/dry sandpaper—600 grit

Damp cloth

Tools

Scissors

Pasta machine

Ruler

Cutting blade

BASSE-TAILLE ENAMEL
RECIPE ON PAGE 125

Instructions

1. To assemble the accordion book, cut the sheet of paper lengthwise, making three equal strips. You can trim them later if they're not perfect.

2. Fold the stack of three strips in half. Open the folded strips and fold each side back toward the center. At this point, you can easily trim the top and bottom edges if necessary.

3. Starting at one end, fold each section in half once more, accordion-pleating so that each successive fold goes in the opposite direction. The finished block should be approximately 1½ x 3 inches (3.8 x 7.6 cm). Separate the strips and arrange them so that the first and last pages of the adjoining sections overlap. Glue these overlapping pages together to make a continuous strip.

4. To create the front cover, roll a sheet of black clay through the pasta machine on the thickest setting. Texture the back of this sheet with corrugated cardboard for visual interest, if desired.

5. Create the faux enamel transfer as directed in the recipe, and trim it to approximately the same size as the folded pages, 1½ x 3 inches (3.8 x 7.6 cm), leaving a slight border for framing.

6. Apply the finished transfer to the smooth side of the front cover, leaf side down. Press lightly and evenly.

7. Cut strips of equal widths from a medium thick sheet of black clay, using the ruler as a guide. Frame the transfer with these strips,

applying them so they lie partially over the image and partially over the raw black clay. Press well.

8. Trim the edges of the frame to butt against one another, and smooth the seams. Cut the framed transfer and backing to its finished dimensions, checking it against the folded pages for proper sizing.

9. Roll another sheet of black clay through the thickest setting of the pasta machine for the back cover, and texture if desired. Cut a rectangle the same size as your finished front cover.

10. Lay a piece of oven-safe ribbon across the back book cover and cover it with another rectangle of textured clay approximately the size of the folded paper accordion. Press well to adhere the ribbon.

11. Bake the covers at 275°F (136°C) for 25 minutes.

12. When the covers are cool, wet-sand any rough outer edges with dampened sandpaper, but be careful not to sand the transfer. Wipe clean with a damp cloth.

13. Glue the pages onto the baked covers and let dry. Tie the ribbon around the book for a closure.

GALLERY

Luann Udell, *River Stone Necklace*. 2001. 29 inches (73.7 cm). Faux river rock with silver findings.
Photo by Jeff Baird

Celie Fago, *Untitled*. 2002. 7 inches (17.8 cm). Carved faux jet bracelet with precious metal clay and sterling silver.
Photo by Robert Diamante

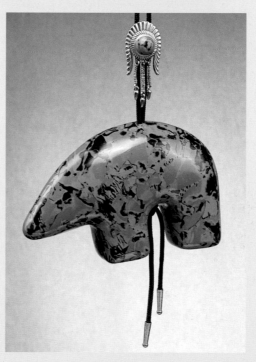

Diane Villano, *Big Bead Series: Zuni Turquoise Bear Fetish*. 2001. 7¼ x 4½ x 2¼ inches (18.4 x 11.4 x 5.7 cm). Faux turquoise over a papier-mâché form.
Photo by William K. Sacco

Celie Fago, *Untitled*. 1999. Pendant 4 x 1⅝ x ³⁄₁₆ inches (10.2 x 4.1 x .5 cm). Carved faux jade necklace with antique brass spacers and glass beads. Photo by Robert Diamante

Irene Semanchuk Dean, *Ancient Coins*. 2002. 1½ inches (3.8 cm). Textured, embossed, and antiqued faux bronze. Photo by Irene Semanchuk Dean

Kim Cavender, *The Hands of Time*. 2002. 5½ x 5½ x ¼ inches (14 x 14 x .6 cm). Faux ivory with distressed and antiqued finish. Photo by Cam Harmon

Deborah Anderson, *Untitled*. 2002. 4¾ x 3 inches (12 x 7.6 cm). Faux leather, carved and tooled. Photo by Liv Ames

Alison Ingham, *Amber Necklace*. 2002. Necklace 17½ inches (44 cm); beads 1 inch. (2.5 cm). Faux amber beads with wire wrapping. Photo by Michael O'Dell

Diane Villano, *Big Bead Series: Peruvian Ceramic Relic*. 2002. 3¾ x 3¾ x 3¾ inches (9.5 x 9.5 x 9.5 cm). Carved, inlaid, and back-filled polymer clay over a wooden form. Photo by William K. Sacco

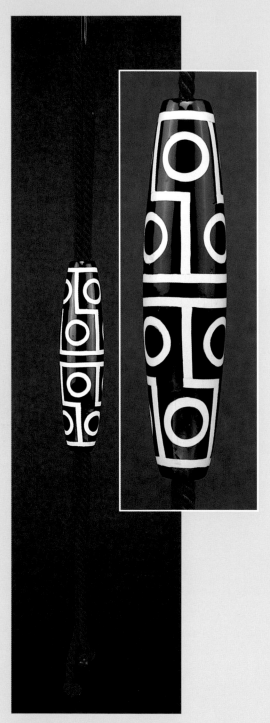

Diane Villano, *Big Bead Series: Inlaid dZi Bead*. 2001. 6¼ x 1¼ x 1¼ inches (15.9 x 3.1 x 3.1 cm). Inlaid polymer clay over a lathe-turned wooden form. Photo by William K. Sacco

Irene Semanchuk Dean, *Three-Legged Bowl*. 2002. 3 x 3 x 6 inches (7.6 x 7.6 x 15.2 cm). Faux jade pinch pot with handformed faux wood legs. Photo by Evan Bracken

Hen Scott, *Ivory Crane Bottle*. 2001. 3¼ x 2¼ x 1 inches
(8.3 x 5.7 x 2.5 cm). Bottle with sculpted faux ivory stopper.
Photo by Archie Miles

Alison Ingham, *number 48*. 2000. 2¼ x ¾ x ³⁄₁₆
inches (6 x 2 x .5 cm). Mixed media pendant with
faux ivory and foiled glass. Photo by Michael O'Dell

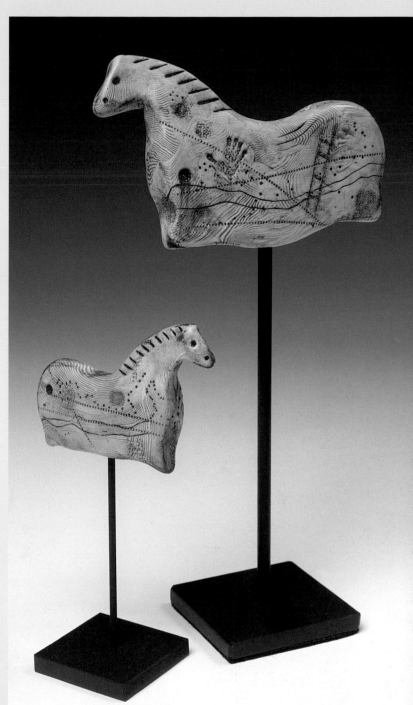

Luann Udell, *Lascaux Horse Sculptures*. 2002. Left, 9 inches (22.9 cm);
right, 16 inches (40.6 cm). Sculpted faux bone artifacts. Photo by Jeff Baird

Irene Semanchuk Dean, *Egyptian Wall Shard*. 2002. 5¾ x 4¼ inches (14.6 x 10.8 cm). Sculpted, stamped, textured, incised, and antiqued faux sandstone. Photo by Evan Bracken

Hen Scott, *Slate Plate*. 2002. 1 x 7 x 7 inches (2.5 x 17.8 x 17.8 cm). Faux slate (textured on stone) with faux verdigris. Photo by Archie Miles

Irene Semanchuk Dean, *Clock*. 2000. 6¼ x 6½ x 3 inches (15.8 x 16.5 x 7.6 cm). Clock with textured faux leather, faux jade with wire wrapping; handbuilt. Photo by Evan Bracken

Hen Scott, *Lapis Mouse Paperweight*. 2001. 1¼ x 1½ x 1½ inches (3.2 x 3.8 x 3.8 cm). Faux lapis lazuli sculpted mouse with molded base. Photo by Archie Miles

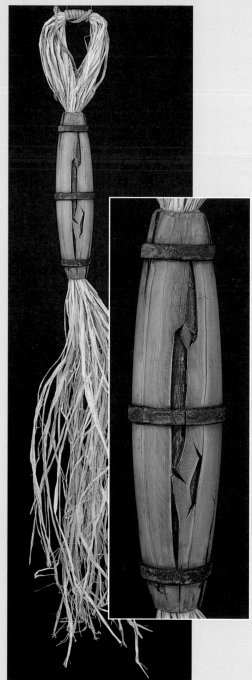

Diane Villano, *Big Bead Series: Fossilized Wood*. 2001. 6 x 1¼ x 1¼ inches (15.2 x 3.1 x 3.1 cm). Faux wood over a wooden form; faux copper verdigris bands. Photo by William K. Sacco

Julia Sober, *Fragment Pendants*.
2002. 3 x 1 x ¼ inches (7.6 x
2.5 x .6 cm). Faux basse-taille
enamel fragments suspended
between microscope slides;
brass and aluminum tubing; and
sterling silver and gold-filled wire.
Photo by Larry Sanders

Gwen Gibson, *Faux Africa*.
2001. Necklace 22 inches (56
cm); beads 1¾ inches (4.4 cm).
Faux sand-cast bronze beads
from a press mold made of rice.
Photo by Robert Diamante

Elizabeth Campbell, *Untitled*. 2002. 20 inches (50.8 cm). Carved faux amber pendant with faux amber beads; earrings with faux amber beads. Photo by Evan Bracken

Artist Profiles

Elizabeth Campbell has always felt the need to "make things." Fortunately, she says, her husband takes care of everything on the planet so she can live in her little crafting world. Her children and grandchildren, too, seem to understand her self-described "flakiness." Elizabeth also serves as the webmaster for Polymer Clay Express (www.polymerclayexpress.com), and loves to write lessons that help other people get started with polymer clay. You can find some of her tutorials at www.sculpey.com and many more at www.polymer-clayexpress.com/lessons.html.

Elizabeth credits a couple of other artists for inspiring her to work with particular faux surfaces—Sally Seiller for dichroic glass, and Cecilia Determan for faience. Contact Elizabeth at elizajc@thepolyparrot.com.

Alison Ingham became hooked on polymer clay when she was 13 and has been making things with it for 18 years; for the last six she has concentrated on jewelry. She has always been influenced by the past—when she was 14, she began painting miniature soldiers for a local company, which gave her a good eye for detail. Alison studied art in Wales, specializing in wildlife illustration, which allowed her to explore her interest in insects. Detail, artifacts, and insects still inspire her; she loves bugs, especially the iridescent green ones!

Alison has a studio at Pastimes Bead Shop in Cambridge, United Kingdom, where she works with polymer clay and teaches workshops. She is a member of the British Polymer Clay Guild, and you can see her jewelry at www.tinymicejewellery.com. Email her at alison.ingham@ntlworld.com.

Instructor and designer **Lynn Krucke** works with many media, including polymer clay; rubber stamps and paper arts; beads and wire; and fabric and fiber arts. Her favorite projects always incorporate techniques from more than one medium. Lynn's designs have been included in books on card making, beading, clocks, glass painting, candles, polymer clay, wearable art, and more. Her work has also been featured in magazines and on websites. Lynn lives in Summerville, South Carolina, and can be contacted at lkrucke@bellsouth.net.

"I always liked art classes in high school and college, but when I found polymer clay in October of 2000, I just fell in love with the medium and have been having so much fun with it," says **Chryse Laukkonen**. "There are so many ways to express yourself with polymer clay." She and her mother, fellow artist Pat Laukkonen, are neighbors and they explore new ideas together. Chryse adds, "My mother is a great inspiration to me!"

Pat Laukkonen was the child of artists and has been drawing and painting since an early age. When she discovered polymer clay two years ago, she found her niche. Even though she has taken art classes off and on all her life, she says none of them inspired her as much as creating something with polymer clay. "This wonderful, versatile medium allows me free rein to experiment with color and patterns in a manner I never thought possible. I'm particularly blessed to share my passion with my eldest daughter," she says, "and her attention to detail has led to the creation of some wonderful faux techniques that we utilize in our designs."

A founding member of the Chicago Area Polymer Clay Guild, **Gerri Newfry** has been working with polymer clay for 11 years. She specializes in the integration of polymer clay and book arts, and markets her work online at www.newfry.com. She teaches classes for the local guild and at art stores. Gerri finds her inspiration in time-honored collage, paper, and book processes.

Pat Pettyjohn began her adventure in polymer clay in 2000. Not realizing there was a large community of polymer clay artists from which to learn, she began to teach herself the endless possibilities of the medium. She now sells her work in galleries and at juried art shows, and periodically teaches classes at a local university. Pat is a member of the Tennessee Association of Craft Artists, the Foothills Craft Guild, and the Blue Ridge Polymer Clay Guild. View her work online at www.CloudyDayStudio.com.

Dr. Heather Roselli is a research scientist turned polymer clay and precious metal clay artist and instructor. She began working with polymer clay in 1995 and precious metal clay in 2001. Her work includes kids' projects, whimsical sculpture, sophisticated jewelry designs, and home décor objects. Heather enjoys the freedom of designing whatever comes to mind and loves the imitative properties of polymer clay. Her designs can be found in magazines, such as *Jewelry Crafts, Belle Armoire,* and *Crafts Magazine*; on websites such as www.sculpey.com; and in the book, *The Weekend Crafter: Polymer Clay* (Lark Books, 2000), by Irene Semanchuk Dean. Her work is displayed on the web at www.WorldofClayThings.com.

Heather teaches classes at the Center for Beadwork & Jewelry Arts and at her home studio, both in Nashville, Tennessee. She is a member of the National Polymer Clay Guild and is a founding member of the Kentucky/Tennessee Area Polymer Clay Guild. Contact Heather at claythings@comcast.net.

An entirely self-taught fine artist, **Dawn Schiller** attended a community college in Illinois for graphic arts training. She moved to California in 1980 to be a "serious artist," and began a career of production art and graphics. She had always wanted to sculpt, but could never quite get the hang of earthen clay; in 1983, an artist friend suggested she try polymer clay—and Dawn says it was a dream come true! In addition to clay, she works with gourds—creating jewelry, spirit gourds, beaded bowls, and figures in the Huichol style—and she continues to do graphics work. Her artwork has won awards for illustration and sculpture, with pieces in galleries on both coasts.

Dawn belongs to the Santa Monica Polymer Clay and Mixed Media Guild, and the Gourd Artisans of Los Angeles (GALA!). She takes classes and attends retreats whenever she's able, always learning new techniques and improving her skills to better realize her artistic visions.

Julia Converse Sober is a part-time mixed media artist and teacher living in Rockford, Illinois. Her discovery of polymer clay in 1991 set her on the path of artistic expression, and she hasn't stopped experimenting and learning since. Since taking her day job running a university radiation safety compliance program in 1996, Julia has delighted in taking advantage of the tuition waiver benefit to pursue an education in jewelry, metalworking, drawing, and design. In addition to teaching and taking classes whenever possible, she has been exploring ways to combine polymer clay with other media, including paper, glass, wire, metal, and found objects. Her love for the endless possibilities afforded by polymer clay have made her an ardent advocate for its elevation to a true art medium.

Julia has taught polymer clay classes for the Chicago Area Polymer Clay Guild and the 2002 *Bead and Button* Show in Milwaukee. She is serving her second term as president of the Chicago guild and loves welcoming new people to the fascinating and diverse world of polymer clay. Reach her at jsober@rocketmail.com.

Luann Udell is a nationally exhibited mixed-media artist. She creates wall hangings, jewelry, and sculpture inspired by the cave paintings of Lascaux, France. Her work is exhibited and sold in fine galleries across the country, and it has been featured in many magazines and newspapers.

Luann attended the University of Michigan, receiving a B.A. in art history and an M.A. in education. From her studies in art history and archeology come the themes that enrich her work—preservation of artifacts, restoration of their context, and interpretation of their meaning. "I imagine an artist of the time the Lascaux cave paintings were created, and strive to make things she would have found beautiful," explains Luann. "And along the way, I find powerful parallels between her time and mine." Luann's studio in Keene, New Hampshire, is a treasure trove of vintage fabrics, antique buttons, and beads. A counter holds drawers and drawers full of rubber stamps, including many hand-carved by Luann. Her book, *The Weekend Crafter: Rubber Stamp Carving*, was published by Lark Books in 2002. See Luann's work at www.durablegoods.com.

Diane Villano holds B.S. and M.S. degrees in art education from Southern Connecticut State University. She is the founding president of the Southern Connecticut Polymer Clay Guild, and teaches and exhibits her work across the country. Her designs have received national awards and have appeared in numerous periodicals and books, most recently in *Making Beautiful Beads* (2002), and Irene Semanchuk Dean's *The Weekend Crafter: Polymer Clay* (2000), both published by Lark Books. Diane can be reached by e-mail at dianev_scpcg@yahoo.com or by mail at Foxon River Design, 1355 North High Street, East Haven, Connecticut, 06512.

A Note About Suppliers

Usually, the supplies you need for making the projects in Lark books can be found at your local craft supply store, discount mart, home improvement center, or retail shop relevant to the topic of the book. Occasionally, however, you may need to buy materials or tools from specialty suppliers. In order to provide you with the most up-to-date information, we have created a list of suppliers on our website, which we update on a regular basis. Visit us at www.larkbooks.com, click on "Craft Supply Sources," and then click on the relevant topic. You will find numerous companies listed with their web address and/or mailing address and phone number.

Acknowledgments

Working on a detailed book like this one requires the talents of many people. The recipe and project contributors provided me with inspired ideas and excellent work, which resulted in a book far more exciting than it would have otherwise been. I'm indebted to my editor, Valerie Shrader, for her considerable organizational skills and editing expertise. My thanks also go to art director Kathy Holmes, who has an easygoing but professional approach, and arranged everything *just so*. Photographer Evan Bracken and I have worked together several times now, and we seem to get better at it each time.

I would also like to thank Victoria Hughes, who pioneered using polymer clay to replicate natural surfaces, as well as the online polymer clay community, whose members are quick to share ideas and discoveries. Lastly, a big thanks to Julia Sober, who knows all the right words.

Index